HIGH MAGIC

IN THE AGE OF

STEAM

A STEAMPUNK'S
INTRODUCTION TO
VICTORIAN
ESOTERICISM

About the Author

Jeffrey S. Kupperman (he/him) is a scholar, artist, teacher, and practitioner. Jeffrey has a master's degree in religious studies from Lancaster University and, having studied religion at Liverpool Hope University, has a Ph.D. in philosophy from the University of Liverpool. He has studied religion, mythology, and magic for over thirty years and has taught college courses in religious studies, theology, philosophy, and anthropology. His esoteric studies and practices range from Freemasonry to Neoplatonism, tarot and traditional astrology, Victorian and Edwardian occultism, and beyond.

He was the founder and publisher of the *Journal of the Western Mystery Tradition* (jwmt.org). He has contributed several papers on kabbalah, tarot, Hermeticism, alchemy, and theurgy and chapters to books on practical occultism and Freemasonry.

When not hip-deep in research, Jeffrey can be found in pursuit of an ever-revolving series of hobbies, special interests, and hyper-fixations. These include icon painting, creating illuminated certificates, martial arts, bookbinding, D&D, designing coloring books, and so on. An avid member of the steampunk community, he can be found at conventions as his persona, the Chevalier Sèitheach MacGregor, the steampunk sorcerer. As such, he can be found presenting on a diversity of topics from necromancy, crossroad curses, talismanry, angel- and demonology, and just about anything from the 6,000 years of religious and occult history he has crammed in his head. He currently resides in central Wisconsin with his children.

HIGH MAGIC

IN THE AGE OF

STEAM

A STEAMPUNK'S
INTRODUCTION TO
VICTORIAN
ESOTERICISM

JEFFREY S. KUPPERMAN

Chicago, Illinois

Paperback ISBN: 978-1-959883-62-3
Library of Congress Control Number on file.

Disclaimer: Crossed Crow Books, LLC does not participate in, endorse, or have any authority or responsibility concerning private business transactions between our authors and the public. Any internet references contained in this work were found to be valid during the time of publication, however, the publisher cannot guarantee that a specific reference will continue to be maintained. This book's material is not intended to diagnose, treat, cure, or prevent any disease, disorder, ailment, or any physical or psychological condition. The author, publisher, and its associates shall not be held liable for the reader's choices when approaching this book's material. The views and opinions expressed within this book are those of the author alone and do not necessarily reflect the views and opinions of the publisher.

Cover design by Wycke Malliway.
Editing by Becca Fleming.
Typesetting by Gianna Rini.

Published by:
Crossed Crow Books, LLC
6934 N Glenwood Ave, Suite C
Chicago, IL 60626
www.crossedcrowbooks.com

Printed in the United States of America.
IBI

CONTENTS

FOREWORD

What you are holding in your hands is something quite extraordinary. It is a little book full of history, wisdom, and anecdotes about the occult revival of the Victorian Age (1837–1901). That in itself, I suppose, does not make it terribly unique. However, in addition to being highly informative, like so many other texts on the subject, it is also highly readable, *unlike* so many other texts on the subject. That alone makes it worth the purchase and the reading.

High Magic in the Age of Steam was written by my good friend Jeffrey S. Kupperman. In part, the book acts as a history text on the occult revival of Western Europe (especially England) in the Victorian Era. However, its chief goal is to assist members of the steampunk subculture in learning about Victorian Age esoteric movements and magic to help them better create believable occult "steamsonas." A "steamsona" is one's steampunk persona for either character play or cosplay. For some, the persona is simply a reflection of a particular aesthetic. For others, it is a complete, magical personality, as real as any other character in a play—if not more so.

For many in the steampunk movement, the assertion that magic was an important part of the Victorian Era may at first glance seem a bit peculiar. After all, was not the Victorian Age the age of advances in science and medicine? The age of industry and technological progress? The age of steam, as it were? Yes, it most certainly was. I should know; I lived through most of it. For many Victorians, however, myself included, these features were only part of the story. Esoteric sciences (Spiritualism, the

study of psychic phenomena, and even magic) were viewed by many of us as an important part of a greater scientific worldview.

In this greater world, it is true, there was no shortage of difficult and unscrupulous individuals, like the hucksters and fraudulent trance mediums who preyed upon the gullible, such as the Islington-born William Eglinton. But there were also incredibly progressive idealists, like Anna Bonus Kingsford, a gnostic Christian who fought for women's rights and animal rights. She, and people like her whom you shall read about in the following pages, were Victorian esotericists who strove to bring a measure of grace and enlightenment to the world.

Victorian occultists were not always the people on the fringes of society, you see, but very often the movers and shakers of the age. Robert Owen, a wealthy industrial reformer and early supporter of the trade union movement, came in his later years in the 1850s to believe ardently in Spiritualism. A gander at the rolls of the Society for Psychical Research, founded in 1882, reveals such luminaries as Sir Arthur Conan Doyle, author of the Sherlock Holmes mysteries, Sir Arthur Balfour, a Conservative Prime Minister, and William James, a preeminent psychologist, among others. Sigmund Freud, Carl Jung, and Mark Twain all supported the goals of the organization, which was to determine scientific methods for authenticating psychic phenomena. The same could be said for the list of names of members of the Hermetic Order of the Golden Dawn in the 1890s, which included people from such respectable middle-class professions as doctor and clergyman, in addition to literary personalities, such as William Butler Yeats, the scion of the Celtic Twilight, and Florence Farr, a West End leading actress, composer, and director.

In short, metaphysical thinking and esoteric possibility were important aspects of the Victorian Age. They are far too often overlooked in favor of its more glamorous materialistic advancements. This book goes a long way toward rectifying this oversight by the steampunk community. It provides a starting point for those steampunks who wish to explore the more esoteric avenues as part of their character development. It is also a starting point for those who wish to delve deeper into the mysteries of the unknown. To those interested in such adventures, I would offer up the following quote from the great scientist Nicola Tesla:

> *"My brain is only a receiver. In the Universe there is a core from which we obtain knowledge, strength, inspiration. I have not penetrated into the secrets of this core, but I know that it exists."*

Courage! brave explorers of the eldritch and arcane! (For what is steampunk, but a realm where we may dream a better world to bring it forth into manifest reality?) May your discoveries of that universal core bring you knowledge and enlightenment!

Professor Marius Mandragore, Esq.
Lammastide, August 2, 2019
Chicago, Illinois

CHAPTER ONE

STEAMPUNK, THE OCCULT, AND PERSONAE—OH MY!

WHAT IS STEAMPUNK?

What does the word "steampunk" bring to mind? I imagine vast seas of goggles uselessly perched on the brims of hats. Others imagine gears. Lots of gears. So many gears. And, of course, science fiction/fantasy meets Victoriana.

The steampunk genre began in the 1970s with an interest in Victorian science fiction, such as the works of Jules Verne and H. G. Wells. The term "steampunk" was meant as something of a joke, playing on the popularity of cyberpunk in the 1980s. It was coined by author K. W. Jeter. Jeter—having written novels based on the widely known universes of *Star Wars, Star Trek,* and *Blade Runner*—tends toward some variation of science fiction. It was when attempting to define his own literary genre that he came up with the term "steampunk."

The point of steampunk being related to Victorian science fiction is important, and for many it is steampunk's defining feature. Steampunk has even been called "Victorian science

fiction."[1] But that definition is too limited, especially given that there is actual Victorian-age science fiction, which steampunk is not. Steampunk has been influenced by Victorian science fiction as a genre, but it also transcends it. Understanding "what is steampunk" is further complicated by its origins in literature. Steampunk can be seen as a genre, or subgenre, of fiction. However, it has hardly remained confined to the page. Steampunks have taken the fandom out of the pages and put it on their bodies, in the décor of their houses, and even in the ways they live their lives. Rather than being limited to a literary and other media genre, as the "Steampunk Scholar" Arthur Slade has eloquently argued, it is an aesthetic.[2]

Aesthetics is an area of philosophy that explores "what is, or should be seen as beautiful."[3] However, aesthetics does not stop at what is "seen." The original Greek word denotes what is taken in by the senses as a whole, and, through the senses, how we understand the world around us and our place in it.[4] This is precisely what Professor Mandragore described in the Foreword to this book. For many, steampunk is an immersive lifestyle that helps the steampunk to experience and navigate the world. And so, we see the goggles, shiny gears, and seas of brown leather, as these things are part of the larger steampunk aesthetic. But an aesthetic goes beyond clothing. People "steampunk" their homes, and they also go to work in nineteenth-century attire,[5] have picnics in cemeteries, and generally live a steampunk life, just like any other punk.

We still find steampunk novels, and a growing number of comics and movies have taken up the stylings of steampunk as

---

1   Cf. Hewitt 7.

2   See Slade, "Steampunk as Aesthetic."

3   See page 8 of Alexandra Grieser's and Jay Johnston's, "What is an Aesthetics of Religion? From the Senses to Meaning-and Back Again."

4   *Aesthetics of Religion* 2.

5   That's me. I'm people.

well. *The League of Extraordinary Gentlemen*, for instance, draws from the aesthetic in both its graphic novel and movie forms. However, not all have taken up steampunk in an obviously English or European context. The kung fu movies *Tai Chi 0* and *Tai Chi Hero* are excellent examples, both drawing on the aesthetic, but reimagining it outside of, and against, European culture. Other steampunk settings exist in entirely new worlds and histories.[6] We even see steampunk applied to other fandoms—the number of steampunk Doctor Who and Harley Quinn cosplays is fantastic, and the more recent series of *Doctor Who* has incorporated steampunk elements into the TARDIS. It seems that anything can be "steampunked" by adding that certain Victorian flair.

Nevertheless, the connection between steampunk and science fiction and science fantasy remains strong. Dirigibles, phlogiston and aether, Tesla guns, and the nearly ubiquitous but often unused goggles and gears, all bring to mind some form of science. As an aesthetic, however, the explicitly late nineteenth-century focus of steampunk outweighs its debt to science fiction and fantasy. By this, I do not mean that all steampunk is, or should be, set during some equivalent of the Victorian era. It certainly should not be set within the confines of Victorian England. Instead, it is the Victorian-era aesthetic that is dominant, even if dropped into a twenty-first-century setting.

What, then, is steampunk? Slade defines steampunk as an aesthetic that mixes three features: neo-Victorianism, retrofuturism, and technofantasy.[7]

Neo-Victorianism refers to an era more than a location—it doesn't have to be English. The people of Ireland, France, Germany, America, India, China, and so forth hardly disappeared during the reign of Victoria. To varying degrees, all these different peoples were talking to one another and thus influenced one another.

---

6   See Slade. These do, however, still tend to be Eurocentric.

7   Ibid.

Photos of nineteenth-century Japan show this quite well, with traditionally dressed geisha standing beside Japanese politicians dressed in Western-style frock coats and high-collared shirts. But *neo*-Victorianism goes beyond this. It is the Victorian era reimagined with modern sensibilities. Because, while there is much to admire from the Victorian era, racism, classism, questionable medicine, and all other evils of the day were still alive and well.[8] There is no need to bring those aspects of Victorian culture into steampunk, there is enough of that in the present day. Also, while steampunk is hardly utopic, there is often a theme of improvement—not only of technology but of society—and bringing the evils of Victoriana into today does not represent a step forward.

Retrofuturism is a particular way of looking at the past; not how the past actually was, but a romanticization of the past. For instance, there were, so far as we know, no functional nineteenth-century jet packs, but we can apply a neo-Victorian aesthetic to such a thing and envision what one might look like and how it might be powered. Perhaps it would be gilded scrollwork and wood and brass framing, and it would run on the mysterious substance known as phlogiston, which for a time people believed actually existed. We also enjoy the comforts of modern bathrooms and are generally in favor of vaccines over bloodletting. Retrofuturism and neo-Victorianism appear to be the heart behind steampunk.[9] But then what of science?

Science, either as science fiction or science fantasy—Slade's technofantasy—is still the primary focus of steampunk today and is what many say separates steampunk from "gaslamp" as a genre. Whereas steampunk is a form of science fiction or fantasy, gaslamp explores themes of occultism, magic, and the supernatural. Like steampunk, gaslamp is often set in a retrofuturistic framework and neo-Victorian aesthetic.

---

8   Okay, some of that hasn't really changed, but science fiction and fantasy often strive to be greater than how we presently are.

9   See Slade.

Certainly, the Victorians were interested in science, scientific advancements, and all the toys and comforts science brings with it. But the Victorian interest in science did not rest solely upon what we consider science today. Victorians also had a deep interest in the occult and occultists—any number of whom were also scientists—and often considered various occult practices as kinds of science. Once the occult is understood as a science, the distinction between steampunk and gaslamp as genres becomes difficult, and there is little, if anything, that distinguishes their aesthetics. There is equally little to prevent either steampunk or gaslamp imagery from intruding on its cousin genre. Such settings are still cohesive, without any tension between the genres of science and magic, though it might exist within the narrative. An excellent example of this is the 2023 MAX animated show *Unicorn: Warriors Eternal*, which seamlessly blends magic and science.

The presence of occultism in steampunk is not meant to disregard or replace technofantasy. While numerous scientists of the era rejected everything concerning the occult, not all did. Members of the Society for Psychical Research, which included a number of physicians, employed scientific methods to investigate the abilities of mediums. Theosophists saw their esoteric interests as being a kind of spiritual science, and they approached their practices in a regimented, controlled, and well-documented manner. The early Edwardian occultist Aleister Crowley[10] even gave his occult journal, *The Equinox*, the motto "The Method of Science, the Aim of Religion." The language of science finds its way into occultism as well, with discussions of magical "energy" and subtle "anatomy." There is also a long history of scientists having serious interests in the occult. Sir Isaac Newton, a practicing laboratory alchemist, is perhaps the most common example.

Steampunk occultism should not, however, be relegated to just another kind of technofantasy. Victorian occultism stands

---

10   Rhymes with "holy."

on its own feet. An occultist from this era may not reject science, but they wouldn't necessarily rely on its findings either, especially where they conflicted with their own occult experiences. The occult has always been part of steampunk, either artificially partitioned as gaslamp, or just generally ignored by steampunks outside the various occult communities. The point of this book is not to redefine steampunk but to expand it to be more inclusive.

To that end, this book consists largely of histories, a steampunk's best friend next to leather conditioner. These histories are introductory in nature; any one of them can fill books, and many have. Many of the following chapters include biographies of important figures within different esoteric traditions so you can get a better feeling for the kinds of people engaging in them. Character sketches can also be found, to help in imagining what various steampunk occultists might look like.

HIGH MAGIC

The term "high magic" has generally been used synonymously with "ceremonial" and "ritual" magic to discuss magical practices that came out of the scholarly traditions of the Middle Ages and Renaissance. This includes the Solomonic magic of the grimoires, the works of Henry Cornelius Agrippa, and the visionary magic of Dr. John Dee, as well as various forms of Cabbalah: Jewish, Christian, and Hermetic. Generally speaking, high magic comes out of traditions that require the magician to be able to read and write. Often, they required practitioners to be able to afford expensive magical accouterments and have ready access to a priest, or to be one themselves. This is typically contrasted against "low magic," which comes out of folk and/or pagan traditions, which may or may not contain elements of pre-Christian religion.

These two classifications are oversimplifications. Objectively, the sources of both high and low magic often intertwine and use identical resources. In the popular imagination, however, these are two distinct branches of magical practice. From the ceremonies of Goethe's *Faust* to the high magic of Sir Adam

Sinclair in the *Adept* series of novels, high magic has a strong grasp on our imagination. This was no less true for the Victorians.

But what is "magic"?

Magic is difficult to define. Scholars have approached the academic study of magic, as opposed to the study of magic for practical purposes, in a number of ways. The most well-known of these studies is the work of Sir James Frazer, published in ever-growing editions as *The Golden Bough*.[11] Frazer developed the idea of "sympathetic" magic, the language of which is not commonly used by occultists. Sympathetic magic affects one thing by manipulating something that is "in sympathy" with it. For example, the use of poppets or dolls with a lock of hair or an article of clothing from the intended receiver of the magic. For Frazer, however, this essentially described all magic. Frazer also understood magic as marking a primitive and superstitious phase of human development.[12]

Frazer's approach is interesting, albeit mistaken, in that it posits a sort of advancement of human culture, where one phase eventually replaces the previous ones. Religion isn't supposed to just move us beyond the need for magic. Rather, it should completely replace what magic supposedly does for us, either through establishing different practices or, ideally, through providing a better understanding of the world. Science, in turn, should completely replace magic. Frazer, of course, was wrong, and there is no reason to believe this will ever happen.

Alternatively, magic can be seen as more of a worldview than merely a (superstitious) practice. The magical worldview exists in opposition to the disenchantment of the world that the Romantic movement of the late eighteenth century tried so hard to fight. This view recognizes ancient wisdom as being just that—wisdom—not an outdated way of thinking that must be replaced. That wisdom, however, is couched in the language of myth and symbol, and it

---

11   The first edition of The Golden Bough consisted of two volumes and the third edition of twelve. Today, there is a one-volume abridged version.

12   See Hanegraaf 716.

must be (re)interpreted every generation so the living, perennial tradition it represents continues.

Victorian occultists fully engaged in this worldview. They looked especially to the ancient Egyptians and Greeks, but also to the grimoires and writings of Renaissance magicians. This view filled the world with spirit, and spirits, in an at least quasi-animist worldview. The old gods, though not always granted full divine status, walked the world, as did angels—including the fallen ones—and elementals. All of this could be accessed if one had the right secret knowledge. This is the knowledge required for the practice of magic, but it was also what was afforded by that which was practiced.

Victorians also understood that magic was a method to spiritually "evolve." While magic was used as a kind of technology to shape the outer world to one's desires, the inner world of the soul was now also available. While this would more commonly be known as theurgy or "divine work" for magical orders such as the Golden Dawn, "theurgy" and "magic" were used interchangeably, with similar exterior practices but vastly different results. Magic deals with changing the outer landscape of the world, and theurgy with the inner landscape of the soul. Even these were considered related, with humanity being a "microcosm of the macrocosm." If you were to watch a Golden Dawn magician engaged in both of these practices, they would look nearly identical.

In the early twentieth century, with the rise in the popularity of psychoanalysis, a new view of magic appeared. In the introduction to *Magic in Theory and Practice*, Aleister Crowley famously defined magic(k) as "the Science and Art of causing Change to occur in conformity with Will."[13] This definition and its variations are still in use today. It can be useful, but it can also be problematic. Crowley purposefully crafted a definition that essentially describes any deliberate act. And that was the point. For Crowley, anything that one purposefully does is magic. This understanding would be modified to fit the new psychological models of thought.

13　See Crowley xii.

Occultist Dion Fortune, who in her mundane life was Violet Firth, a counselor in a psychotherapy clinic, would change the ending of Crowley's formula to define magic as the art of changes in consciousness at will.[14] The purview of magic was now the mind. For some, this didn't change magic all too much. The mind is vast, and changes in it can correspond to changes in the world around us. For others, magic became the new psychotherapy.

Today, practitioners of magic may engage in any and all of the above understandings of the magic art (and science). Beyond these, however, magic also has an aesthetic quality. Magical practice often involves special clothing, the use of magic circles, pentagrams and pentacles, swords, daggers, and so on. Goths, as well as members of the modern Pagan community, have been drawn to much of this, either (or both) as an aesthetic or a practice, and occult symbols can often be found in their jewelry, clothing, tattoos, home décor, etc. Victorian occultists tended to keep their esoteric aesthetics more or less private. One did not see people dressed in fully ceremonial regalia walking down the sidewalk and claiming to be invisible. For the most part, you won't see steampunks doing that, either. However, much like goths or Pagans,[15] adding esoteric elements to one's attire is entirely in keeping with steampunk as an aesthetic. My persona, for example, wears a number of talismans that appear as medals or parts of his watch chain. He has the caduceus of Hermes, god of magic, hidden in his cravat and "spats of the arte," a steampunk play on the magical garters, which gave the magician the ability to travel anywhere in the world, found in the *Greater Key of Solomon*. He also is known to wear a leather wizard hat on occasion and has tarot cards tucked into the band of his top hat.

This esoteric aesthetic has had enough impact that it has begun influencing pop culture. Shows like *The Order*, and books like *The Magicians* and *The Dresden Files*, have made use of it in varying ways. *The Irregulars*, a one-season, steampunk-inspired, show

14 See Butler 16.
15 Goth, Pagan, and ceremonial magician are in no way mutually exclusive categories.

on Netflix, combined steampunk, the occult, and a world based loosely around Sherlock Holmes, is another excellent example. Episode three featured a magical order based on, and named after, the Order of the Golden Dawn. The names of the members were only slightly changed to protect the guilty. The episode mixed Victorian and esoteric aesthetics, and a beautiful tarot deck that was, disappointingly, made only for the show.

DON'T EXPAND THE EMPIRE!
Or Appropriation, Stolen Valor, and Why That's Bad

Empires, in general, come about through conquering other peoples and taking their stuff. It generally doesn't matter which empire it was or when or where it existed—someone was conquered and their stuff was stolen. "Conquered" might be by social rather than military means, and "stuff" could be physical or cultural in nature, but the analogy holds. Culture, or cultural practices, cannot be stolen in the same way a car can be stolen. The term most commonly used is "appropriation." Cultural appropriation is taking something that does not belong to us, such as a cultural practice considered "closed" by the culture to whom it belongs, and twisting it to fit our needs and desires, often without reference to its originating cultural significance, and sometimes purposefully in opposition to that significance. Understanding just what this means, and what it does not, can be tricky.

Part of the difficulty is the nature of cultures themselves. Cultures are not static, monolithic, or "pure" things. They flow, they change, and they interact with other cultures, borrowing from them and being borrowed from in return. To varying degrees, whenever a people come in contact with another, some form of cultural exchange and change always occurs. With this give-and-take element, which exists with any group of people in contact with another, it seems like the idea of appropriation, of taking elements of a culture to which one is not entitled, makes little sense.

And this would be true if all peoples met and exchanged as equals, but this is simply not the case. Many cultures have expanded through the use of force, military, religious, economic, and otherwise. In such situations, where the power imbalance is extreme, the movement of culture, or cultural practices and beliefs, is controlled by the imperialist. When this happens, elements are appropriated from the colonized culture, taken without reference to how they exited in their native form, becoming like a bauble to be played with and put—or thrown—away when interest wanes. That is, appropriation flows in the direction of the powerful and lacks respect for the practices and beliefs that are appropriated. This means appropriation is a very specific kind of act. Engaging with practices and beliefs that do not come from your own culture, religion, or whatever, is not automatically appropriation. A good rule of thumb is that if the culture, country, etc., actively and *freely* export some element of itself, then feel free to partake. The Scottish kilt is a good example of this. The Scottish government actively promotes its wear to non-Scots, and there are numerous, registered, nonclan tartans. However, this is not infallible. When dealing with cultures that have been, at some point, under European rule but are now self-governed, determining what is freely given, what was coerced, and what was taken and now just looks like it was given can be tricky.

The traditions discussed below are living traditions. There are still Spiritualists, Theosophists, and Golden Dawn magicians. In the United States alone, there are over a million Freemasons. The Theosophical Society, Golden Dawn, and Freemasonry actively and publicly promote their beliefs and practices through both official publications and the publications of members. Building a steamsona with elements drawn from any of these traditions should be done respectfully, whether or not you, personally, subscribe to any of their beliefs. The information in this book will help you do that. These traditions have also drawn from other cultures, and not always in a respectful manner. This is especially true when it comes to Hindu and Buddhist traditions, which were often viewed through the lens of Orientalism. This distorts Middle Eastern,

Southern Asian, African, and East Asian cultures and peoples in such a way as to make "the East" seem exotic, mystical, romantic, and barbaric in comparison to "the West."

Stolen valor is when someone claims a rank, degree, or honor to which they are not entitled. Many of the traditions and organizations discussed are initiatory in nature, and/or have specific secrets, grades, and privileges associated with them. An Adeptus Minor of the Golden Dawn, a Master Mason, and a Martinist Free Initiator are people who earned their grades and titles. This can represent years of study and the practical application of those studies. That is, they are earned, not simply taken and claimed.

There are steampunks with personas in the clergy, with military rank, dukedoms, and so on, where the person behind the persona isn't clergy or in the military. Is this stolen valor? Based on two principles, I suggest it is not. First, these titles are usually taken with some amount of respect to them. We don't tend to see people who are violently opposed to the military taking military ranks in order to denigrate them. Second, and possibly more importantly, the actor behind the character is not making any claim to those titles. A steampunk dirigible crew may refer to one another by rank, and there may even be some expectation that other steampunks respect the fiction of those ranks. However, we're all aware that those ranks are held by the persona and not necessarily the person. The person is not misrepresenting themselves to be something they are not.[16]

This is important to keep in mind when developing and performing your steamsona, especially because you will eventually encounter steampunks who are actually entitled to the ranks and degrees your persona claims. Most likely, they'll play along. That's part of the fun. But outside of the immersive world of steampunk, your persona's Master Mason degree isn't going to be recognized by any Freemason. You wouldn't expect actual service members to

---

16 When in doubt, you can invent honors, degrees, and secret orders as you need them.

salute you, let alone discuss military operations with you, because you do military reenactment. The same holds true in steampunk. Also important is to recognize that there is a difference between *appropriation* and *appreciation*. In cases of appropriation, practices, clothing, symbolism, etc., are taken and used without particularly caring about what those things might mean to those whom it is being appropriated from, whether they consider it a closed practice, or really anything else. Appropriation is about taking, and it need not make any reference to where whatever was taken came from. Think of the Borg from *Star Trek*. Appreciation takes into consideration all of these things. If you appreciate a culture or a practice, you don't just take it because you like it. You learn about it, what it means, whether or not the culture it comes from is okay with people from outside engaging with it, etc. If the practice is closed, like the Jewish seder or the *Tā moko* tattoos of the Maori, then appreciation means *not* engaging in something when that something isn't for you. To continue the *Star Trek* metaphor, think of the Federation.

Don't be the Borg.

MOVING FORWARD
INTO THE PAST

When possible, I have attempted to arrange what follows in something resembling a chronological order. We will start with Spiritualism, which leads directly into the development of the Theosophical Society, which indirectly leads to the creation of the Order of the Golden Dawn. However, history cares naught about the tidiness of this book. Freemasonry predates everything else discussed by several hundred years, and Martinism is at least a hundred years older than the magical orders that arose during the Victorian era. However, high magic, as represented by the Golden Dawn, the Hermetic Brotherhood of Luxor, Martinism, and so on, were heavily influenced by Freemasonry in ways which Spiritualism and Theosophy were not.

I've tried to create a flow leading from Spiritualism, which started in the mid-nineteenth century, to the most popular forms of high or ceremonial magic in the late nineteenth century. In some instances, this means playing the role of a chrononaut and jumping around the timeline. Also, the discussion is not necessarily limited to the nineteenth-century history of any of the traditions discussed. We will look at eighteenth-century Masonry and Martinism as well as some twentieth-century Pagan practices. This is so you can better see how occult currents develop over time. This will be valuable when you start creating your persona, but also if you choose to develop something new, which partakes of bits and pieces of these traditions.

A WORD ON TENSE

Part of the difficulty of writing this book is the issues of tenses—past, present, future. Everything that is discussed below continues to exist. As such, there will be things that both were and are taught, practiced, and believed. When writing of these as they occurred in the nineteenth century, I will generally use the past tense, even if they are still present today. When discussing these traditions as they are today, I will endeavor to use the present tense, even if what is being discussed comes from an earlier period.

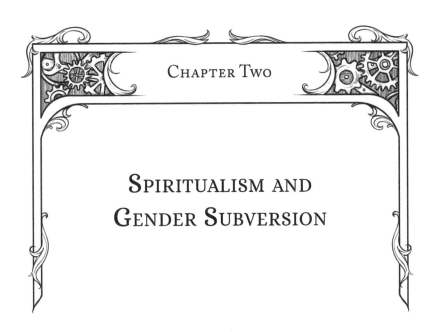

CHAPTER TWO

SPIRITUALISM AND GENDER SUBVERSION

A BRIEF INTRODUCTION

Spiritualism, unlike many other religions, has an oddly specific beginning: March 31, 1848, in Hydesville, New York. This is when and where the Fox sisters claimed to have made contact with the spirit of a salesman who had been murdered and buried in the cellar of their home.[17] Margaretta, called Maggie or Margaret, and Catherine, called Cathie or Kate, were twelve and fourteen years old at the time, the daughters of John David and Margaret Fox, and younger sisters to future medium Leah Fish. What began with mysterious rapping sounds would develop, first in the United States, and later in England and Europe, into a religion dedicated to contacting the spirit world. But Spiritualism was also committed to women's rights, abolitionism, and the overthrowing of oppressive religions and social institutions.

Spiritualism, however, was not birthed in a vacuum. Although the Fox sisters were the locus of the first spiritualistic phenomena

---

17 No evidence of this murder has ever been found.

that would act as midwife to the religion, they are not exactly the beginning of Spiritualism's story. At least four streams fed into the river that is Spiritualism: Swedenborgianism, mesmerism, New Thought, and Quakerism. Much like Spiritualism, these all exist and are practiced today.

Most of the early Spiritualists were Quakers who had left the Society of Friends, as they called themselves, having felt it had moved too far from its original doctrines. Quakers taught that the divine spirit of God is present in all people. This indwelling spirit is the source of spiritual authority and religious truth. Tradition placed authority in the meetings of the Society of Friends which ensured Quakers met the rigorous standards of their morality and lifestyle. There was an inherent tension between this and the doctrine of the inner light that gave each Quaker spiritual authority. For instance, even before the Civil War, there were Quakers who were prompted by the inner light to speak against the buying and selling of enslaved people who were silenced by the rigid structure of the Society's meetings. The individual and the meeting, directed by Quaker elders, could not both have authority.[18]

In 1827, Elias Hicks would lead a schism in the Society of Friends. Hicks and his followers believed the authority of the individual should outweigh that of the meetings. The Hicksites would break away from the original Society's meetings to form their own group, which often advocated abolitionism. Even this new forum proved too restrictive for some Quakers, such as those who engaged in antislavery activities with non-Quakers. Activities with non-Quakers were forbidden in both the Society of Friends and amongst the Hicksites. These Quakers quickly separated themselves from the Hicksites, becoming the Congregational Friends. Isaac and Amy Post, close acquaintances with the Fox family, helped form this new Society in Waterloo, New York.[19]

---

18   See Braude 12–13.

19   Ibid. 13.

The Congregational Friends held the Quaker ideals that all humans had within them the inner light of God and were created in God's image. Because they believed each person was "a limited transcript of the perfect Architect," it was understood that "an unbroken chain of communication" existed between God and all other beings.[20] As we'll see, Spiritualists held a similar view, with the dead transmitting messages from the afterlife to the living.[21] Further, Spiritualists held that anyone, though especially women, could receive these messages, regardless of social class or race.

Where Congregational Quakerism was the moral and spiritual foundation of Spiritualism, Swedenborgianism was its intellectual heart. Swedenborgianism, translated through the New Thought of Andrew Jackson Davis, provided Spiritualism with much-needed metaphysics and philosophy. Emmanuel Swedenborg was an eighteenth-century military engineer, zoologist, philosopher, and theologian.

In his mid-fifties, Swedenborg developed psychic abilities and began having spiritual visions of heaven and hell, which Davis would further develop in a way that directly influenced Spiritualism. Swedenborg also introduced the idea of a subtle, though still physical, substance called "ideoplasm,"[22] which can be seen as the forerunner of ectoplasm. The idea of ectoplasm was used in the early 1900s to explain the source of the now-common rapping phenomenon made famous by the Fox sisters.[23] Ectoplasm was discovered by Dr. William J. Crawford, a lecturer in mechanical engineering in Ireland in 1914, and studied and named by Dr. Charles Richet, a French physiologist, making for wonderful examples of the mixing science and the occult.

There were some mixed feelings toward Swedenborg's theology amongst Spiritualists. Swendenborg's theology was founded on

---

20   From Waterloo Friends, Proceedings, as quoted in Braude 13–14.
21   See Weisberg 13–14.
22   Ibid. 16.
23   Ibid. 113.

his belief that he had received the secrets to the Second Coming of Christ. It included whether or not one remained married after death, the nature of the Trinity, which exists only in Christ, and a rejection of the Lutheran idea of salvation through faith alone. Sir Arthur Conan Doyle, the famous author and well-known Spiritualist, thought it was too arbitrary. According to Conan Doyle, Swedenborgian scriptural interpretation turned everything in the Bible into symbols, and usually symbols that were completely counterintuitive to the seemingly plain meaning of the text. In other areas, it was too extreme or internally contradictory.[24] These were not the parts of Swedenborgianism that would come to influence Spiritualism. Instead, Swedenborg's visionary experiences of heavens and hells would become the basis for Andrew Jackson Davis's metaphysics.

Davis, the founder of the New Thought movement,[25] would become the prophet of "Harmonial Philosophy" and the author of *The Principles of Nature, Her Divine Revelations, and a Voice to Mankind*, in which he would attempt to synthesize and explain Swedenborg's teachings. Davis was not simply approaching this as an intellectual endeavor. He claimed to be in contact with the soul of Immanuel Swedenborg himself, which he attained through mesmeric trances.[26]

Swedenborg's original vision of hell and heaven consisted of six spheres, three hells and three heavens, each one progressively worse or better than the one before it. Spiritualists would come to reject the existence of hell, especially American Spiritualists, who would reject mainstream Christian churches and their teachings about sin and evil. Davis "corrected" Swedenborg's model by claiming all the spheres were, in fact, heavenly. However, the sphere directly after the Earth was more chaotic than the more spiritually refined spheres that followed, arguing that

---

24 Conan Doyle 14–15.

25 New Thought is not the focus of this book. For more, see Henry Harrison Brown, New Thought Primer, "Now" Folk, 1903.

26 See Braude 34.

Swedenborg misinterpreted this as hell because of its chaotic nature.[27] According to Davis, beings from any sphere could, and did, make contact with mediums.

In the United States, Spiritualism typically defied attempts at universal organization. The nature of American Spiritualism, which emphasized individual freedom, did not allow for such organizations, though they did occasionally exist on a small scale. In England, Spiritualists, who typically rejected organized religion less than their American counterparts, were more readily given to forming organizations. Such groups were often formed and governed by upper-class Spiritualists, but also often attempted to mitigate British classism, looking to preserve the rights and interests of all. The American emphasis on individuals and rejection of organizations had widespread influence outside of Spiritualism.

OF THE VARIETIES OF MEDIUMS

Mediums, the majority of whom were women, were typically divided into four types.[28] The first was the private or close circle medium. Such a person, often of the middle- or upper-class, would operate in a small circle, usually of friends and neighbors. Many such mediums relied on rapping sound, such as were first manifested by the Fox sisters, to relay spirit communications. The raps were purportedly caused by the spirits of the dead by manipulating the ectoplasmic body of the spiritualist. They were used to answer simple yes or no questions but could also relay more complicated information. For the latter kind of communication, Isaac Post, the Fox sisters' early benefactor, introduced a system involving the recitation of the alphabet after the medium asked a question.[29] The spirit would knock when the appropriate letter was reached and the alphabet was

---

27   See Braude 40.

28   See Owen 174–175.

29   See Braude 11–12.

then recited again for the next letter in the message. The process could be performed relatively quickly, with the medium rushing through the alphabet as fast as she could, but for longer answers, this was still a time-intensive process. The Ouija board would obviate its need.

The second and third kinds of mediums were both public in nature but did not perform their mediumship in the same ways. These mediums were often from a lower socioeconomic class and, unlike the close circle mediums, they would often charge, directly or indirectly, for their services. The first of these were lecturers, who became popular in the 1850s and 60s. Such lecturing mediums entered a trance state and, through this passivity, channeled a soul from one of the spiritual spheres and gave speeches on various subjects. Topics included the afterlife but spirits would also frequently lecture on suffrage and women's rights in general, and, at least in the United States, abolitionism.

The second kind of public medium gained prominence in the 1870s and were akin in appearance to stage magicians, who often resented the competition. These stage mediums caused the rapping sounds, but also spirit manifestations. Through stage mediums, spirits could move objects from one place to another, even between rooms, completely unseen. Spirits could also appear to non-mediums during sessions. Such appearances could be anything from a pair of ghostly hands, a face, or an entire body. In general, special conditions, such as a dark room, were necessary for these manifestations, but this was not always the case. Manifestations were more common amongst American spiritualists than their European counterparts.

Unlike lecturing mediums, stage mediums would often withdraw into darkened spaces, sometimes specially made cabinets, and this was understood as the only way the manifestations could occur. This marks something of a change from the earlier lecturing mediums. Spirits no longer possessed or spoke through their hosts. Now they could appear directly. Also different from earlier Spiritualists, many of these stage mediums did not engage in social reformation movements. Their cause, rather than equality between the sexes, was a defense of mediumship itself.

The distinction between the kinds of mediumship was not always clear. Some close circle mediums would also create spirit materializations. Florence Cook, who became a medium in 1870, was able to produce such manifestations, but she also showcased the more usual spirit raps amongst friends in the Dalston Association, a close circle of spiritualists in London who specialized in training new mediums. Once Florence became associated with the mediums Charles Williams and Frank Herne, she came into contact with a "spirit control" named Katie King. This spirit would, as happened with lecturing mediums, take control of Florence. At this point, spirit manifestations became Florence's primary effort as she transitioned from her close circle to stage performance.[30]

In England, a fourth kind of medium was not only common but also greatly revered: the healer medium.[31] The rejection of mainstream medical practices appears to have gone hand in hand with the rejection of other institutions that stifled female autonomy. In America, it was generally considered that women were becoming less healthy over time and those opposed to women's rights believed a woman's reproductive organs naturally tended toward disease. Spiritualists, among other health reformers, argued that it was society that caused illness and a woman's body naturally tended toward health.[32]

The ability to heal was found amongst mediums of all social classes and was part of both private and public mediumship. Numerous healing practices, such as homeopathy, hypnotism, the laying on of hands, and most especially mesmerism, were drawn into a medium's healing resources and were combined with spirit intervention. Such healers were also deeply concerned with creating a rapport with their patients. These relationships

---

30   See Owen 44–47.

31   Ibid. 107.

32   See Braude 142.

were more intimate than those of mainstream medical practices[33] and were part of the overall Spiritualist ideology that rejected top-down relationships that gave complete control to the physician.

Healing mediums were also found in America and, on both continents, women dominated the field. Although they did not seem to hold the same level of prestige as their British counterparts, American healers used similar techniques, including clairvoyant trances to diagnose a patient.[34] Both British and American healers worked to distinguish themselves from mainstream medical practitioners. They denounced the use of purgatives, stimulants, and narcotics, instead relying on "natural" remedies in combination with their mediumistic abilities.[35] Spiritualist healers, although generally available for all who needed them, also often focused on women's health issues and women's health reform.[36] This can, once again, be seen as part of Spiritualism's larger agenda of female autonomy.

SOCIAL ACTIVISM

Victorian Spiritualism was not simply an intellectual activity or social parlor trick without repercussions outside of the investigations and lectures. Both American and European Spiritualists were interested in women's rights, including suffrage and the right for women to own property. Another Spiritualist social interest was freedom from marriage. This took the form of working for the right to divorce as well as the right to not get married in the first place. American Spiritualists, with Spiritualism's emphasis on equality, were also interested in abolition,[37] a subject less important to English Spirituals as slavery had been abolished in England in 1833.

---

33 See Owen 109–110.

34 See Braude 146–147. Cf. Owen 109

35 Ibid. 147. Cf. Owen 109.

36 Ibid. 151.

37 See Braude 56.

Although there was universal agreement amongst American Spiritualists on the need for women's suffrage and the ending of slavery, there was no agreement on which was more important. In either case, it was often women—such as Mary Fenn Davis, whose husband was the aforementioned Andrew Jackson Davis—who led the way in both of these distinct but related movements, amongst Spiritualists and non-Spiritualists alike. Mary Davis quickly became more important than her husband as a spokesperson for both abolitionism and women's suffrage.[38]

The Spiritualists and non-Spiritualists involved in both did not always work well together. Non-Spiritualists, for instance, were often concerned with how their movement looked to those who did not believe in Spiritualist claims. Spiritualists often thought the Spiritualist message should be at the forefront of these movements.[39] In some ways, however, the non-Spiritualists needed Spiritualist involvement. Spiritualists brought in numbers their non-Spiritualist counterparts could not;[40] there were simply more Spiritualists than non-Spiritualists in either movement. Spiritualists were also often more active than the non-Spiritualists. For instance, Spiritualists continued to agitate for women's suffrage during the American Civil War, while non-Spiritualist involvement lapsed.[41] The focus on abolitionism also saw the rise of prominent Black Spiritualists, such as Sojourner Truth, Rebecca Cox Jackson, and Harriet Jacobs. Unfortunately, Black Spiritualists are grossly underrepresented in writings on the subject.

Healing mediums were also engaged in women's rights activities, mediated through their "medical" practices. As mentioned previously, such mediums had a distinct focus on women's health, although they would treat anyone, regardless of class or gender. This was at the same time when regular practitioners, including medical doctors and the new alienists (the psychologists and

---

38 See Braude 58.
39 Ibid. 70–73.
40 Cf. Braude 73.
41 See Braude 79.

psychiatrists of the time), were increasingly seeing women as the physically and psychologically weaker sex. Even mediumship would be classed as a form of hysteria and was connected especially to female biology. It was often seen as a form of religious delusion, which was also often associated specifically with women.[42]

Trance and clairvoyant healing mediums rejected such diagnoses. They believed women were naturally very strong. It was, they claimed, a systemically sexist society that caused women much of their problems. History has, of course, borne this out. The healers, for their part, besides their use of mesmerism, homeopathy, spirit healing, and herbalism, engaged in a less hierarchical healing practice, giving patients more control over their treatments. In America, such mediums were also often involved in dress reform movements, which saw the dresses, petticoats, and corsets women were required by society to wear as unhealthy. Andrew Jackson Davis, for instance, promoted "practical dress reforms" and the "American costume," which consisted of bloomers or a short skirt over loose trousers[43] rather than many-layered dresses. Spiritualists like Davis saw the common clothing mores for women as not only regressive but as a form of slavery. Dress reform, as well as health reform, were closely connected to the primary Spiritualist message of equality and personal freedom and were seen as necessary components of an overall spiritual lifestyle.[44]

ENTER CULTURAL SUBVERSION

Although it was believed that anyone, of any age, could become a medium, the demographics were weighted toward working-class women. It was also more common for young women, or even preteen girls, to become mediums than older women, though age did not limit a medium's abilities once manifested. But why women?

---

42   See Owen 142–144.

43   See Braude 151.

44   Ibid. 152.

At this time, women in the United States and Britain had little influence outside the house, had no right to vote or own property, and had even fewer rights once married. Even inside her own household, a woman's influence was questionable, as philosopher Mary Wollstonecraft showed in her writings on women's rights.[45] Unlike the popular view that the woman ran the home while the man was at work, a married woman didn't necessarily have control of the home she was expected to take care of. Instead, her husband not only controlled the expenses but also micromanaged their wife's management of the home. She might have taken care of the home and children, but she did so in accordance with her husband's requirements. The reason for this being the common idea that women were simply less intelligent and less morally inclined than men, and so needed their guidance. This was an ideology to which Wollstonecraft not only strongly objected, but neatly took apart in her writing.

Given the authority mediums would hold within their circles, both public and private, and their role in gaining women's rights and influencing abolitionism, one might think more men would have taken prominent roles. While men did often play an important role in getting female mediums access to public forums, the importance and authority of women far outstripped that of male Spiritualists.

Spiritualist groups, especially in the US, were also sometimes involved in the free love movement.[46] Although this might be seen as a natural extension of the women's rights stances of Spiritualism in general, and especially the fight for women to have the right to not get married, this element of Spiritualism does not appear to have ever become popular in England. Nevertheless, Spiritualism's romance with free love does make sense. American Spiritualists staunchly supported ideals of personal freedom, reflecting the

---

45 See Wollstonecraft, A Vindication of the Rights of Women.

46 This is by no means true of all Spiritualists; according to Braude (129), most rejected it. Those who were involved in free love were seen as being even more "radical" than other Spiritualists.

Quaker roots of the Congregational Friends. Even amongst Spiritualists who rejected free love, marriage, which gave both the woman and her property to her husband, was seen as immoral and possibly irrevocably corrupt. The free love movement saw itself as being in opposition to the discriminatory institution of marriage. Its opponents, though, saw it as a license for promiscuity. To varying degrees, both sides were correct, and in either case, free love meant a rejection of the social mores accepted by the majority of the populace.[47]

Not all proponents of free love completely rejected marriage. Anne Denton Cridge, for instance, desired both autonomy and a family and sought a compromise between the two. This was necessary as she could not, in nineteenth-century America, acceptably have a family without also being married. If nothing else, marriage increased the odds a woman with children would not be left to raise them alone when the man who fathered them disappeared.[48] This also shows the diversity within Spiritualism. There was no single Spiritualist view on marriage, love, the nature of the afterlife, or even the nature of mediumship itself. Also, although Spiritualists often disagreed with one another on how to go about getting what they wanted, Spiritualists possessed a proven ability to talk with one another about their disagreements, and Spiritualism's roots include strong support for free speech.[49]

The influence of free love, or even less radical notions connected to female autonomy, while explainable, also may seem somewhat contradictory to other aspects of Spiritualism. For instance, the cultural elements of women's suffrage and abolitionism were part and parcel of Spiritualism, while the gendered metaphysic upon which Spiritualism was grounded was based on what should seem like a less woman-friendly, not to mention less woman-dominant, ideology. Following what is perhaps now a well-known system of thought, men were seen as being more positive or forceful

---

47 See Braude 127–128.

48 Ibid. 131–132.

49 Ibid. 129.

and women as negative or passive. Women, at least "proper" or upper-class women, were seen as naturally moral and chaste as well, especially when contrasted with men or the working class. This view of the "womanly woman" was at least in part modeled on the Christian idea of the Virgin Mary as the new Eve, whom women should emulate as far as possible. Although this was typically used as an ideological force against women's rights, in the context of Spiritualism, this idea made women the perfect candidates for becoming mediums—the perceived feminine passivity and goodness were exactly what made women the best mediums. Further, women who often could not read, or were generally un- or undereducated, were exemplars of the lecturing medium. No one would believe an uneducated, working-class woman could have the ability to stand and speak on their own, sometimes for hours, before an auditorium of educated gentlepeople, let alone lecture eloquently and intellectually on complex topics. Several well-known women mediums made substantial livings doing exactly this.

In this lay a paradox. Women were the main force of Spiritualism. Women were the ones through whom the spirits spoke, gave their messages, and proved the existence of an afterlife—one very different, and often more attractive, from what the Protestant Churches of the time preached. Women were the gatekeepers to such messages and teachings, but at the same time, those messages did not belong to or come from the mediums who conveyed them. Even the way in which mediums worked was subject to this paradox. It was a man, often one of education and social position, who would act as a manager for or would "run" a lecturing medium's lecture as a sort of master of ceremonies. The medium would enter a passive trance state and allow the spirit to speak through them, often saying afterward that they had no memory of the subject of their lecture. From at least the public's perspective, men ran the show. The medium was merely the conduit through which the performance occurred.

The question was whether or not the women were what they seemed. This could be taken in a number of ways. The most obvious concern was fraud. Many mediums were debunked as such. The famous stage magician, Harry Houdini, became interested in Spiritualism after his mother died, and he debunked several mediums after finding frauds when trying to contact his mother—some of whom coincidentally had shows more popular than his. Accusations of fakery and the use of stage magician-like techniques were not uncommon.[50] Even earlier, the press waged a battle against Spiritualism's authenticity,[51] specifically that of the Fox sisters during their rise to fame.[52] Even Maggie Fox, in an attack against her older sister Leah in 1888, and possibly as a way to stave off starvation due to poverty, denounced Spiritualism as false, the mediums as frauds, and its followers as foolish fanatics.[53] She would recant this confession the next year.

As Spiritualists also engaged in healing practices, claims of fraud were also common from the mainstream medical profession. Medical professionals had been watching healing mediums from early on, as well as Spiritualism in general. They were not impressed, and alienists tended to regard Spiritualism and its claims as a form of lunacy and linked female mediumship to hysteria.[54] Healing mediums were even occasionally brought to trial for fraud, such as London's Dr. Henry Slade.[55]

There may have been, however, another kind of illusion being perpetrated by women Spiritualists: the passivity associated with mediumistic trance may have been fraudulent. This does not mean the mediums themselves were necessarily frauds, but there is no reason to think mediums, both those who would escape from a working-class life, or a middle- or upper-class wife in bondage to a husband who would control her property and life, would not see their activities as a medium as a path to some form of emancipation, be it social, financial, or both.

---

50 See Dyson in Kontou and Willburn 246–247.
51 See Weisberg 122.
52 Ibid. 124–126.
53 Ibid. 239–240.
54 See Owen 139.
55 See Braude 159.

This perhaps represents the greatest of Spiritualism's cultural subversions. Mediums were able to use social norms, which existed to subjugate women to male dominance, to free themselves from that dominance. Spiritualism provided women an outlet for their own autonomy. It also enlisted men, who may have seen themselves as being in charge of their seemingly helpless and passive medium wards, to help in this endeavor. Such men may have even been effectively, unbeknownst to themselves, placed in the passive position of following the medium's presumably spirit-directed promptings while "their" medium was really in charge of her activities. The manager did the work of putting together sittings and lectures, the medium made money and acted freely in a way other women could not.

The popularity and influence of Spiritualism would eventually wane but would never entirely vanish. Spiritualist churches still exist today, especially in England. Spiritualism would also influence Helena Petrovna Blavatsky, one of the founders of the Theosophical Society, which would in turn influence many esoteric movements and traditions afterward and continues to do so to this day.

FRAUDS

As mentioned before, there were frauds. Some mediums didn't know they were frauds, believing they were having mediumistic experiences while, instead, they were simply just good at cold reading people. Others, however, knew they were fakes, and strove to make whatever money they could by putting on seances, psychic readings, and other events. Various spiritualist camps also formed networks where information was shared so as to be better able to take advantage of people who frequented spiritualist readers. Once a sitting was booked, word would go out to other camps to see if a mark had visited any of them, and information about them was sent to the camp in question. Harry Houdini made a reputation for himself debunking frauds. Unfortunately, he also "debunked" a number of genuine mediums.

CHARACTER SKETCH: THE SUFFRAGETTE MEDIUM[56]

Ms. Francisca Stone hails from the East End of London, having grown up in the remnants of the wealthy parts of the district, and she now resides in New York City. Having agitated for votes for women at home, she has taken to organizing local cells of women for the same cause in the States. It was in New York that she met a small circle of mediums meeting in Queens. Through this group, Ms. Stone was able to unlock her own abilities as a healing medium. Ms. Stone works as a healing consultant with her close friend and…roommate, Dr. Jennifer O'Toole. She also reports on politics for a local Suffragist newspaper, *The Weekly Sunflower.* Her column is called "Suffrage at Home and Abroad."

Ms. Stone is shown here in the so-called "American costume" of loose-fitting pants and a jacket with a number of pockets, rather than petticoats, skirts, and a corset. The ensemble could be in any color, but steampunk's favorite color palette consists of shades of brown. She proudly wears a "Votes for Women" sash, which would have been in white, purple, and green. Here the "steampunking" of the outfit is subtle: her earrings are small Ouija board planchettes and her knee-high leather boots, rather than shoes, have several pockets worked into them.

---

56 See Appendix B for a more in-depth look at the personae presented throughout this book.

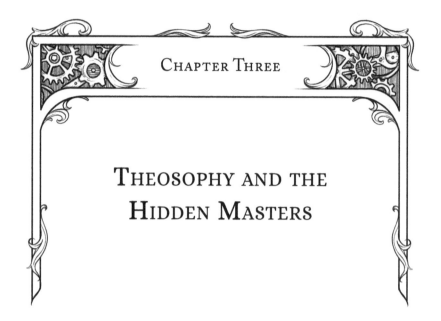

CHAPTER THREE

THEOSOPHY AND THE HIDDEN MASTERS

On November 17, 1875, in a rented hall in New York, Madame Helena Petrovna Blavatsky oversaw the Theosophical Society's inaugural address. This was presented before a small gathering of women and men by Colonel Henry Steel Olcott.[57] Olcott proposed the formation of the Theosophical Society (TS) for the purpose of studying psychic and occult phenomena, as well as mysticism, Cabbalah, and other forms of esotericism.[58] Blavatsky, however, was the Society's main inspiration and driving force.

"Theosophy" comes from the Greek words *theos* and *sophos*, "God's wisdom," and predates the TS's use of the word. Olcott understood it to mean "wise in things of God." The theosophy of the Theosophical Society is a philosophical and esoteric system that was born from, and a response to, Spiritualism. Blavatsky saw it as a reformation of Spiritualism.[59] The TS's approach to Spiritualism was meant to move away from its Quaker and Swedenborgian roots—at least that is what Blavatsky claimed. For

---

57 See Gomes 1.
58 Ibid. 85–86.
59 See Lavoie 9.

her, theosophy was the revelation of an ancient religious wisdom tradition, even if it was one that often asserted many of the same beliefs as Spiritualism.[60] The TS would eventually branch into the study of other forms of esotericism, especially those brought from India by European and American imperialists, as well as genuine spiritual seekers. However, its original purpose was to provide philosophical underpinnings for Spiritualism, much as Andrew Jackson Davis had done decades earlier. Where Davis would look to, and "correct," Swedenborgianism, the TS would first look to the Neoplatonists and Cabbalists before shifting its gaze East to Hinduism and Buddhism.

Although the influence of Spiritualism on Theosophy's initial development is clear and well-documented, the members of the Society, especially Blavatsky, saw the teachings of the Theosophical Society as being part of a more ancient tradition. This metaphysical position is known both as the *philosophia perennis* and the *prisca theologia,* the "perennial philosophy" and "ancient divine knowledge."[61] Blavatsky assured one Professor Corson of Cornell University that the teachings of the TS came from long before the Fox sisters' first raps. Their roots were the same as those of the astrologer Raymond Lully, and of Neoplatonists and Cabbalists such as Giovanni Pico della Mirandola and Henry Cornelius Agrippa.[62] All this implies the Theosophical Society's theosophy was no new development, but part of an ancient lineage of wisdom traditions dating to antiquity, a theme common to Victorian-era esoteric societies. This ancient wisdom was understood to be universal, and variations occurred due to cultural differences in its diffusion. Each of these distinct strands, however, could be traced back to a "pure" wisdom tradition. This, in turn, was maintained by "Hidden Masters," pure and advanced souls who communicated with a chosen few, such as Blavatsky, to perpetuate the *philosophia perennis.*

---

60 See Lavoie 9.

61 Ibid. 169.

62 See Cranston 117–118.

It was typical for such occult societies, as the Theosophical Society styled itself,[63] to express this universal wisdom in terms of Western esoteric traditions, especially Neoplatonism and Hermeticism, as well as a Christianized form of Jewish mysticism, Cabbalah. As a result, for a time, the Theosophical Society followed suit. Ultimately, though, the members of the Society would settle on an Eastern ideology for its presentation of the *prisca theologia*. However, above and beyond seeing itself in line with Eastern or Western mystical traditions, the Theosophical Society defined itself as being occult, and in this way, it saw itself differently than Spiritualists did.

By "occult," members of the TS meant that they could directly change the world around them. This was accomplished by affecting the subtle or metaphysical worlds the physical world was situated in and derived from, most commonly termed the "astral fluid" or "light." Whereas Spiritualist mediums passively received communications from the spiritual realm, Theosophists could actively communicate with those denizens with proper training, and, through the application of their will, change the physical world around them.[64]

Causing beneficial change in the physical world through applying a proper metaphysical understanding, what Blavatsky referred to as "white magic,"[65] was only one of the aims of the TS. A further aim, which it shared with Spiritualism, as well as the *philosophia perennis* in general, was a kind of spiritual "evolution" or perfection. Blavatsky believed that true occultism was not to be conflated with the so-called occult arts, such as alchemy, astrology, and magic. True occultism, or *Atma Vidya*, in the later Indian-influenced language of the TS, is "knowledge of the soul." A true occultist was one who acted for the benefit of the

---

63   See Lavoie 169.

64   Ibid. 172.

65   See Cranston 31.

world rather than themselves and did so by acting through their higher or divine self rather than the selfish ego.[66] Through many incarnations, the soul was believed to perfect itself and become a Hidden Master, a Bodhisattva-like figure.[67] With a foot in both worlds, Theosophists tried to align the physical world with the spiritual.

MADAME BLAVATSKY

Unlike Spiritualism, which began with the Fox sisters and ultimately transcended them, Madame Blavatsky remained, and remains, Theosophy's central figure, even though others would eventually take up the mantle of leadership after her death in 1891. To best understand the TS, and those drawn to it, understanding Blavatsky and Colonel Olcott is necessary. In this, the influences of Spiritualism on Theosophy, and where Theosophists rejected elements of Spiritualism, will be better understood.

Perhaps above all things, Blavatsky being a feminist should not be surprising. The Spiritualism she grew up around and in drew upon feminism as much as it did the supernatural. Her grandmother, Helene Pavlovna Dolgoruki, who came from Russian aristocracy, was well-educated, well-read, and a great influence on her granddaughter's early life. Blavatsky's mother, Helena Andreyevna Hahn von Rottenstern, was equally refined and also a feminist. Although her mother died while she was still young, von Hahn's influence on her daughter was unmistakable. The feminism and support for women's suffrage that was part of Blavatsky's worldview,[68] as well as her burgeoning psychic abilities, invariably led her to Spiritualism, which did not simply embrace such ideas, but celebrated them.

---

66   See Cranston 31–32.
67   See Lavoie 172.
68   Ibid. 15–16.

At the age of seventeen, Helena Petrovna married Nikifor Vladimirovich Blavatsky, a man about twice her age, though Blavatsky would later claim he was seventy, rather than forty. Like her mother, a novelist, Blavatsky had a gift for the imaginative and was a known taleteller. Blavatsky would leave her husband after about three months of marriage. Rather than settling into married life, Blavatsky traveled to the Middle East, Turkey, Greece, Egypt,[69] the Americas, India, England, Russia, and Tibet. She wasn't simply sightseeing. Blavatsky had a longing to learn the spirituality of the places she visited, especially those of India and Native American communities.[70] By the time she reached New York City in 1873, twenty-four years after leaving Nikifor, she was broke, possibly had a child out of wedlock, and was distraught after two unsuccessful relationships. It was there, in New York, that she entered the world of American Spiritualism.[71]

Spiritualism's allure to Blavatsky, now forty-two years of age, should be obvious. Blavatsky was a feminist, a suffragist, and a psychic. Spiritualism was like coming home, at least for a time. Blavatsky was a self-avowed Spiritualist, at least during the years between her arrival in the United States and the founding of the Theosophical Society three years later.

It is possible she was "converted," as she said, to Spiritualism in Paris by Daniel Home in 1858,[72] long before her arrival in New York City. Home was a noted Scottish Spiritualist, known for being able to levitate chairs and tables.[73] Home's writings suggest they never met, and by 1876, the two seem to have hated one another.[74] This is possibly due to an affair between her, a commoner despite her grandmother's lineage, and Prince Emil

---

69   Ibid. 18–19.
70   See Cranston 48–51.
71   Ibid. 22.
72   Ibid. 35–36.
73   See Gomes 21.
74   Ibid. 95–97.

zu Sayn-Wittgenstein-Berleburg between 1857 and 1858, which purportedly resulted in the birth of a child who died in 1868.

Regardless as to how she became a Spiritualist, by February of 1875, Blavatsky had become disillusioned by the number of fraudulent Spiritualists she had encountered, though, at the time, she still connected her *philosophia perennis* to Spiritualism. Eventually, she would deny she had ever been a Spiritualist at all. This isn't to say Blavatsky denied mediumship, psychic abilities, or any of the phenomena associated with Spiritualism. She fully affirmed these, and her own psychic abilities, which included forms of telepathy, mediumship, and materializations, were well accounted for. It was Spiritualism itself, at least as she encountered it in the 1870s, that she rejected as being full of frauds and unscientific in practice. The Theosophical Society, being dedicated to the scientific and exacting exploration and teaching of psychic and occult abilities, was to be a remedy for this.

COLONEL HENRY OLCOTT

Henry Steel Olcott was born in 1832, two years after Blavatsky, in New Jersey. Although not descended from royalty, the Olcott family could trace itself back to at least the sixteenth century, with the first "Olcott, Thomas," arriving in the New World in the early seventeenth century, some ten years before the Mayflower. Olcott was the son of God-fearing Presbyterians,[75] and it was this Presbyterian background, the conservativeness of which Olcott rejected, that would lead him to Theosophy, and eventually to Buddhism. And, as important as he is to Theosophy, he is perhaps even more important to Theravada Buddhism, so much so that he is honored by Sri Lankan Buddhists every year on February 17, and by Indian Buddhists on February 2, the day of his birth.[76]

In his youth, Olcott, unlike Blavatsky, was hardly a world traveler. When he was twelve, he went to New York to witness the

---

75   See Murphet 1–3.

76   See Prothero 1, 19.

psychic powers of Andrew Jackson Davis. He would also encounter religions as far-ranging as Mormonism, Swedenborgianism, and, importantly, Spiritualism, during his youth.[77] At fifteen, he entered New York University, but he left at the age of sixteen for financial reasons. Although he had business contacts, he instead became a farmer in Ohio. In 1848, Olcott was introduced to the newly budding Spiritualism by his maternal uncles. Olcott became one of the founders of the New York Conference of Spiritualists in 1853 and wrote a dozen or so articles for the Conference's newspaper, *The Spiritual Telegraph*.[78] Olcott would fondly credit this introduction, and more especially his uncles, for placing him on the path toward Madame Blavatsky and the Theosophical Society.[79]

Spiritualism was not Olcott's only esoteric interest. He had a keen interest in mesmerism, which was also influential to Spiritualism. He practiced mesmerism himself and was able to get results from his practice. One notable instance was his use of this art as a local anesthetic for a young girl undergoing dental surgery. After making his mesmeric passes, the girl reported experiencing none of the pain she should have otherwise felt.[80] Olcott would come to be considered a virtuoso healing medium.[81]

Olcott eventually left farming and took up the academic study of agriculture at the Westchester Farm School. This and the study of certain sugar plants, on which he would become an expert, led Olcott to some fame in agricultural circles. After writing his second book on agriculture in 1858, a then twenty-six-year-old Olcott would take his first trip outside the United States on a tour of Europe.[82] When the Westchester Farm School closed, Olcott found himself once again making a fresh break from his former life. He became an editor for the *New York Tribune*,

---

77 See Prothero 19–20.

78 Ibid. 24.

79 See Murphet 4–5.

80 Ibid. 6.

81 See Prothero 23–24.

82 See Murphet 7–8.

which had abolitionist leanings, and a writer for the *Mark Lane Express,* an English corn-trade newspaper. This led to adventures in the American South, and a number of close escapes for Olcott, who was willing to write about anything that would bring some adventure to his life.[83]

It was this sort of adventure, his abolitionist beliefs, and a certain amount of New York pride, that led Olcott, newly married, to join the military as a signals officer in 1861. By the end of 1862, Olcott was awarded the rank of colonel for his work against racketeers attempting to defraud the military. He left active service to become a lawyer in 1868, with a sterling reputation and as an acknowledged investigator.[84] In 1870, the Colonel, as he was still called, traveled to London, only his second time outside the US, where he took to visiting mediums. Olcott would move through a number of other careers and would lose two of his four children to an early grave, and eventually his wife to divorce. But through all this, his interest in the occult never left him.

THE THEOSOPHICAL SOCIETY

Although Madame Blavatsky would always be the central figure of the Theosophical Society, it was the Colonel who proposed its formation and gave its inaugural address in 1874. Together, Olcott and Blavatsky would create a spiritual society still in existence today, though it has seen a number of schisms and offshoots. Given the romanticism of Blavatsky's life, and the far-ranging activities of Olcott's, how they met is somewhat prosaic—he offered her a light for her cigarette.[85] Despite their differences, this seemingly chance meeting, or possibly the working of karma, would spark a long-lasting relationship and a Society which has some 30,000 members.

---

83   See Murphet 8–10.

84   Ibid. 15.

85   See Olcott 1.

The purpose of the Society was to approach Spiritualism from a scientific standpoint, something which Blavatsky considered notably lacking among Spiritualists. Specifically, it was created for the scientific research of "spirit phenomena, mesmerism, Od Force, psychometry, the magnet, occultism, and practical magic."[86] Olcott proposed to form a society of occultists, gather a library, and begin collecting and disseminating ancient knowledge, occult research, and religious and philosophical insights in the chain of succession of the *philosophia perennis*.[87] There was, and is the Society for Psychical Research, which had interests in Spiritualism, and had some members who were Spiritualists, but the SPR was for the purpose of studying spiritual phenomena. The Theosophical Society not only studied such things but taught its members how to practice them. Eventually, the TS would evolve to include Eastern influences, as well as a base of operation in India, and the idea of the Society as a Brotherhood would become one of its cornerstones.[88]

The TS's occult inspiration was originally Western and included an "Esoteric Section" dedicated to the study and practice of Western occultism and magical practice. In 1877 the TS, under the Colonel, took a decidedly Eastern direction. Olcott, in correspondence with one Moolji Thackersey of India, rewrote the brief history of the Society and claimed it had always existed to promote Asian religion and to discredit Christianity in America.[89] Olcott, possibly under the influence of Blavatsky, would write at length against Christianity, something he had not done previously. Blavatsky's book, *Isis Unveiled: A Master-Key to the Mysteries of Ancient and Modern Science and Theology*, also contained anti-Christian material, though the TS, through the

---

86 See Prothero 48.
87 See Olcott 120.
88 Ibid.
89 See Prothero 64.

work of such lights as Anna Kingsford, head of the London Lodge of the TS in the 1880s, would reconcile itself with Christianity, by combining Christ with the future Buddha Maitreya, who was seen as the figure who would save of all humanity. Olcott also believed Blavatsky had Eastern contacts, and to have possibly gained her psychic abilities there. The "East" was, ultimately, seen as the source of "Western" esoteric spirituality and practice. Even the most noted Western occult practitioners of the time, such as Éliphas Lévi, were seen as amateurs and failures as occultists.[90]

Because of this new focus, there is a great deal of Hindu and Buddhist-derived language in Theosophical and related[91] literature. It is questionable as to whether the concepts behind the TS's technical language follow Hindu and Buddhist thought. There are also strong elements of Westernization to be found. But ideologically, Eastern notions, from a nineteenth-century Orientalist perspective, are still at the heart of the Society's teachings. Even with these Western touches, there are still contemporaneous experts, such as Dr. G. P. Malalasekera of the World Fellowship of Buddhists and noted Zen teacher, D. T. Suzuki, who believe Blavatsky had to have been initiated into some Buddhist sect, or at the least had access to information not otherwise available in the West based on her writings.[92]

Eventually, the Theosophical Society was led not only by Olcott but by prominent Theosophists Annie Besant and William Quan Judge. Judge split with Olcott and Besant in 1895, effectively taking the American part of the Society with him. Judge's Society underwent further schisms in the early twentieth century. Olcott and Besant, the latter of whom was an active Co-Mason, moved their base of operation to India, where it still operates. Rudolph Steiner became the General

---

90   Ibid. 104–105.

91   Such as Alice A. Bailey's books and her Lucis Trust and Arcane School.

92   See Cranston 83–84.

Secretary of the German and Austrian branch of the Society, under Olcott and Besant, in the early twentieth century, and kept his division oriented largely on Western forms of esotericism. Due to disagreements with Olcott and Besant, Steiner split from the TS in 1913, forming the Anthroposophical Society, which still exists and is responsible for the Waldorf Schools.

THEOSOPHICAL TEACHINGS

KARMA

Karma, a Sanskrit word meaning "action," is perhaps the most well-known Hindu and Buddhist teaching in the West. The Western understanding of karma is heavily influenced by Theosophy's use of the term. The Society understood karma as the "law of retribution" which functions to keep equilibrium or harmony in the universe and was not to be seen as reward or punishment. It was specifically transmitted through beings, such as gods or goddesses or various spirits, the agents of the Lords of Karma. Regardless of how karma comes about, it was always in response to our own actions. Karma could affect individuals, families, nations, and entire races, and it linked all people together.[93]

Karma was not attached to the individual, but to the soul, and so not only followed a soul from life to life but was also one of the mechanisms behind reincarnation. This was because karma kept the soul, as well as the ego, linked to physical manifestation. As the soul evolved and shed its karma, it lost the desire to reincarnate. Such spiritual evolution may be marked by forms of initiation and ultimately lead the soul to become a Mahatma or Master.[94] The idea of spiritual evolution was important and fit with other pre-Darwinian notions of evolution, which saw

---

93 See the "Karma" entry de Purucker's Encyclopedic Theosophical Glossary.
94 Cf. Gordon 357–358.

humanity as moving in a definite direction from the primitive to the advanced, physically, culturally, and spiritually. The human soul, especially those of the more advanced "root races,"[95] was thus destined to take its place amongst the Masters.

DEVAS

Following in the line of the *philosophia perennis*, the Theosophical Society taught the existence of many different kinds of spiritual beings and, specifically, a spiritual hierarchy. Generally, these spiritual beings could be described as *devas*, which is, roughly, Sanskrit for "divinities." Such beings may be good or evil or neutral toward humanity and the evolution of creation. There were many different kinds of devas. The most important of these, from the perspective of humanity's spiritual evolution, made up the Hierarchy of Compassion. This consisted of seven classes of being: the *adi-buddha, mahabuddha, daiviprakriti,* and the Sons of Light, as well as *dhyani-buddhas, dhyani-bodhisattvas,* and *manushya-buddhas.*

The *adi-buddha* was the primeval Buddha, the Awakened One above and beyond all other Buddhas. It was a primordial force beyond knowing and understanding. The Masters were the representatives of the *adi-buddha* on Earth. The *mahabuddha* was the "great consciousness," the mind of the cosmos. The *daiviprakriti* was the first matter emanated by the cosmic mind. This was not matter in the physical sense of the word but the spiritual lattice upon which physical matter is based, similar to the idea of "etheric"[96] matter and the Aristotelian *hyle*. The Sons of Light made up numerous other spiritual hierarchies and were often associated with the planets and stars, which were spiritually understood to have been from the *daiviprakriti*. The *dhyani-buddhas*, the Buddhas of Contemplation, consisted of seven beings,

---

95   See the Races section in this chapter.
96   See the Subtle Anatomy in this chapter.

each associated with one of the seven ancient planets. They gave us our divine kings and prophets; those who teach humanity the sacred arts and sciences which lead us toward spiritual evolution. The Bodhisattvas of Contemplation sprang from the minds of the *dhyani-buddhas* and, like their progenitors, led humanity upward. These were purely spiritual or nonhuman beings. The *manushya-buddhas* were human buddhas, typically Mahatmas, and were connected to the seven root races. The most well-known of these is Siddhartha Gautama, the historical Buddha.[97]

Mahatmas

Of all the Society's teachings, perhaps its most important was that of the Masters or Mahatmas, meaning "great self." The Masters, an idea that still exists in the TS, its various offshoots, and their numerous New Age movement grandchildren, were spiritually advanced beings, sometimes human, sometimes incarnate, sometimes not, who guided true esoteric organizations. By the early 1900s, such organizations would become known as being "contacted," meaning they were not just led by its human hierarchy but had a direct link to spiritual beings and worked toward the spiritual evolution of humanity. They were the links in the chain of the *philosophia perennis*.[98] Olcott would credit the Mahatmas for the teachings in Blavatsky's monumental *Isis Unveiled*, and Blavatsky herself, though she would come to regret it, did the same.[99]

A number of Masters were known by name, or at least aliases, such as Koot Hoomi, Hilarion, and Morya. Koot Hoomi was important to the founding of the TS, even if Blavatsky and the Colonel didn't know it at the time. Correspondences purportedly from him were the foundation of Theosophist A. P. Sinnett's *The*

---

97 See de Purucker.
98 See the "Master(s)" entry in in de Purucker.
99 Cf. Cranston 151–152.

Mahatma Letters to A. P. Sinnett. Master Morya was Blavatsky's guru, and both he and Koot Hoomi were from India, although Masters were found in the Himalayas, China, Japan, India, and other places.[100] The Mahatmas were not just a passing Theosophical fad. They would guide the TS through a number of successors, as well as provide new ancient teachings to the Society and its members. The Mahatmas would find their way, as Secret Chiefs and Ascended Masters, into later esoteric, and not-so-esoteric traditions, and are still popular in various New Age movements, almost all of which may be considered Theosophy's grandchildren.

SUBTLE ANATOMY

Subtle anatomy was the theory that all things have multiple bodies, not just the gross physical one. Of these, perhaps the most well-known was the astral body. Each subtle body had different properties and existed or functioned on different, but interwoven, planes of being. There were numerous systems of subtle anatomy, each with different numbers of bodies, as well as names for those bodies. Madame Blavatsky combined elements of Vedanta and Western esotericism to develop three subtle bodies: the *mayavi-rupa* or "Illusion body," the *Linga-sharira* or astral body upon which the gross material body was based, and the *karanopadhi,* the causal body that was the vehicle for the higher mind of the soul.

Annie Besant and C. W. Crawford, later leaders of the TS, expanded upon Blavatsky's original bodies and changed their names. Between the physical and astral bodies was placed the etheric body, which was now seen as the template upon which the physical body was based. The ethereal level was considered material or physical as well, but more subtle, hence the designation of the physical body as the "gross" physical body. The astral

---

100 See Cranston 82–83.

body was now the body of desire and the vehicle of the emotions or the irrational soul. Beyond this was the mental body which was related to the rational mind. The causal body remained the most refined and was associated with, or was the vehicle for, the abstract, higher mind.

Initiation

When one thinks of "initiation," images of college hazing might come to mind, but so might images of lavish ritual dramas. This was certainly true of Freemasonry and the ceremonial traditions discussed in the next chapters. In such organizations, initiations took the candidate through a ritualized drama, often involving an oath or obligation, and was given the various secrets of the grade, such as passwords, handshakes, and the like. Not so in Theosophy.

While there was an implied, and often explicit, spiritual dimension to the initiations of Masonry and the like, the Theosophical Society did not necessarily engage in initiation rituals, though it did recognize initiation rituals of other traditions. For the TS, initiation was a purely spiritual phenomenon. For the Theosophist, the soul alone underwent initiation, which was the means through which the soul evolved from its most basic level to becoming a Mahatma. Theosophy taught that there are seven levels of initiation. The first three prepared the initiate for the work to be done. By the time the fourth degree was reached, the initiate was aware of their inner god, or higher self, and began to experience the other planes of existence. In the fifth degree, the initiate met their inner divine principle. The sixth-degree initiate had transformed themselves into a vessel for that divine self, and the seventh degree was the awakening of the Christ-self and eventually the awakening to Buddhahood through the attainment of Nirvana.[101]

The TS also taught that with each spiritual initiation, a series of trials was presented to the initiate that transpired

---

101 See the "Initiation" entry in de Purucker.

through the events of their everyday life. The successful passing of these events meant the aspirant was ready to attain the next level of initiation. Otherwise, the initiate had found their current place in their spiritual evolution and should work on the lessons necessary to continue that evolution. This idea should be approached cautiously, as it can easily become a kind of spiritual victim blaming, with the negative events of one's life being reduced to "spiritual trials" and not being "evolved" enough to surmount them.

RACE

The Theosophical theory of race was possibly the most problematic of the Society's ideas. In its Victorian form especially, it was little more than a spiritualized form of racism. This idea carried through the history of the TS, as well as a number of its offshoots, especially the works of Alice A. Bailey. Lamentably, it can be found in some modern Theosophical writing as well, though it has in some cases evolved to divorce itself from its earlier racism. This idea held that different races had evolved on the planet, taking the form of root races, each of which consisted of numerous other races. Each root race was seen as being more spiritually evolved than the last. After a race reached its spiritual potential, it gave way to the next race, though traces of previous races may remain on Earth for some time. Some Theosophical writers, such as Bailey, saw Africans and Jews as representatives of earlier, spiritually less evolved, root races, with the Aryan root race being the most spiritually evolved.

The Theosophical Society's ideas about race were wildly popular. Unfortunately, this led to their inclusion in Nazi ideology and, ultimately, the Shoah or Holocaust. This ideology is still found in some esoterically inclined White supremacist writings, as were some popular Theosophical books, though most of modern Theosophy has moved away from the racist interpretations of the late nineteenth and early twentieth centuries.

CHARACTER SKETCH

Here we reach the problem of appropriation discussed earlier. India has spent a significant portion of its recent history under English rule, which makes figuring out what is freely exported and what was just taken somewhat difficult. Further, India is also a frequent destination for spiritual tourists of European descent. That said, the wearing of saris or a bindi are not generally considered closed practices. That is, they are open to anyone to partake of, and, done respectfully, can be well managed. "Can we" and "should we" are, of course, entirely different things. So, I hesitate to create what might be an appropriately Indian-influenced character sketch. Anything I could create would pale in comparison to what someone of Indian descent could do.

CHAPTER FOUR

FREEMASONRY, TEMPLARISM, AND THE ROSE + CROIX

The subject of fraternal societies falls somewhat outside the topics of the previous two chapters. This is not because of the overall subject matter, as we'll see such societies were, and are, involved in social issues, and in many instances, have strong esoteric interests. What is different is that fraternal organizations, especially Freemasonry, the primary focus of this chapter, are much older than Spiritualism, let alone the Theosophical Society. Victorian Theosophy was influenced by—and a reaction against—Freemasonry, and so one might expect this chapter to precede the others. However, our focus here is not on fraternal societies in general, but their influence on the Victorian world, esoteric or otherwise.

There are many different kinds of fraternal societies. Many may be familiar with academic fraternities and sororities, usually denoted by various combinations of Greek letters. There are also service societies and those that can only be entered by having the correct family lineage. The societies about which we're concerned do have some similarities with these other organizations. However, they are also different, often substantially so, such as with their distinct interests in moral development, the pursuit of philosophy,

the study of religion, and very often, esoteric or occult elements.[102] Most of these societies are, or were, as the name "fraternity" suggests, for men only. This is not always the case, and even some traditionally male-only fraternities have transformed to allow women or have women-only cognates.

The (Ancient) Free and Accepted Masons is one of the most well-known and oldest of such fraternal orders. The earliest records of what is most like modern, or "speculative," Masonry date to the early-to-mid 1500s and are from Scotland, with English references occurring shortly thereafter.[103] Outside of claims to the perennial wisdom, claims which many esoterically oriented fraternal societies make as well, we can see that speculative Masonry predates both Spiritualism and Theosophy by several hundred years.

Like Spiritualism, Masonry has a strong concern for social justice and equality amongst all people. Like Theosophy and Spiritualism, many Masons, even if not Masonry itself, have an interest in the occult. Masonry's structure, and its habit of collecting from the intelligentsia, royalty, and the politically powerful, provides an ideal setting for the interests of its members. The Masonic Lodge acts a locus for the study and practice of the occult, as well as engagement in social and political activities; topics that intertwine more than one might think.

A BRIEF HISTORY OF A LONG TRADITION

Speculative Masonry possibly developed from operative masonry as early as the fourteenth century. Operative masonry was the work of practicing stone masons, such as those who built the famous medieval cathedrals. At some point, wealthy non-operative masons were accepted into operative masonic guilds. These non-operative Masons would eventually transform the tools and traditions

---

102 Other such societies may also use occult symbols, but they are often for shock and aesthetic affect rather than for esoteric study.

103 McIntosh 63–64.

of operative masonry into allegorical lessons, set in a narrative surrounding the building of King Solomon's Temple. This was seen as the "scientific application and the religious consecration of the rules and principles, the language, the implements, and materials of Operative Masonry to the veneration of God, the purification of the heart, and the inculcations of the dogmas of a religious philosophy."[104] Speculative Masons would eventually outnumber operative masons within their own guilds, leading to masonry's transformation into something like what is known today as Freemasonry.

The most popular, or at least populous, form of Freemasonry can be referred to as "malecraft Masonry," as only men may join. The first three degrees, which were the core of Masonry, were together sometimes referred to as "Blue Lodge" Masonry. The color blue represented the expansiveness of the heavens, which a Mason's mind should imitate. This was the attitude inculcated in the three degrees of Masonry proper,[105] and during the Victorian era, at least in England, it was so distinguished from the "red" degrees which followed.[106]

It was usually claimed that Blue Lodge Masonry came into being in 1717. Which, as we've seen is entirely incorrect. Rather, Masonry took the form by which it is now known by 1717. This was when the Grand Lodges of London and Westminster were formed by several smaller lodges. In 1813, these combined with the Ancient Grand Lodge of England, a rival set of lodges to form the United Grand Lodge of England (UGLE). Craft Masonry consisted of three degrees: Entered Apprentice, Fellow Craft, and Master Mason, which imitated, with the addition of the third degree, the degrees of medieval Operative Masonry. Each degree engaged the Mason with certain moral teachings. These were propagated through allegorical stories and the symbolic use of Operative Masonic tools, such as the well-known square

---

104 See Mackey's Encyclopedia entry on "Speculative Masonry" (Vol II, 704).

105 See "Blue" in Mackenzie (Vol I, 76).

106 Ibid. "Blue Masonry" (Vol I, 76).

and compass. The constitutions of the UGLE also included the Royal Arch degree, wherein the Master Mason's secret Word was learned, although this is now typically part of Red Lodge Masonry.

The Grand Lodge system was the norm in Masonry, with most countries typically having a single Grand Lodge over all the individual regional lodges. The Grand Lodge had a constitution and bylaws that regional lodges followed. Freemasonry came to the United States as early as 1715. The first American Grand Lodge was formed after the Revolutionary War, with George Washington as its first Grand Master. Each state would come to have its own Grand Lodge, which would typically recognize the Grand Lodges of other states. As with their European counterparts, each state Grand Lodge oversaw the operations of its local lodges.

Masons moved through the degrees through a series of oral examinations and dramatic initiatory rituals. The rituals were performed from memory and took the candidate through a series of symbolic trials, culminating in a drama set in the building of King Solomon's Temple. Each ritual had several officers with ritual titles such as Junior Deacon, Senior Warden, and Worshipful Master, who is in charge of the Masonic Lodge for the given year.[107] It is during these rituals that the moral teachings of Freemasonry were first imparted. These were reinforced through the study of degree-specific material as well as participating in the initiations of other Masons.

Besides the rituals, Freemasonry was distinguished by its costume. Unlike Spiritualism or Theosophy, where special ritual clothing was not required, Masons were most well-known for their white lambskin aprons. The aprons of Master Masons, and especially those of Worshipful or past Masters, were often elaborately decorated. Decorations might include symbols such as the square and compass, the all-seeing eye, the two pillars from the porch of Solomon's Temple, a skull, and so forth. Traditionally,

---

107 "Worshipful" here does not mean, as anti-Masons would have you believe, that the Master of the lodge is literally worshiped. Rather, worshipful can be seen as similar to "venerable," typically used in France, or "honorable."

Masons dressed as well as they could for Lodge meetings, though some orders had specific ritual clothing, so the sight of suits or military uniforms was not uncommon during lodge meetings. In Red Lodge Masonry, which consisted of appellate bodies that work degrees past that of Master, aprons might contain other symbols, and other modes of dress, such as the distinctive Templar uniform, would be worn.

Also worn were various "jewels," a kind of pendant that symbolically represented an office. For instance, the Worshipful Master wore a square, which was symbolic of morality and honor.[108] Officers of a Grand Lodge may wear a chain of office. Different degrees in the appellate rites had their own jewels and sometimes medals. For instance, the medal of the Knight Rose Croix degree took the form of a pelican feeding its young on its blood, a symbolic reference to Christ, contained within a compass over an arch, suspended from a red ribbon.[109] The Knights Templar degrees of the York Rite also had such medal-like jewels.

SOCIAL TRANSFORMATION

Freemasons, in the time of Victoria as well as today, saw the Craft as existing to strengthen the moral character of individual Masons through the application of the Socratic virtues to their lives, a dedication to the divine, however the Mason might view it, and the charitable relief of those in need. In short, Masons saw themselves as trying to transform the world into a better place through both self-improvement and charitable acts.

The requirements to become a Mason were relatively few: be of good report, be able to afford dues, and believe in a Supreme Being, the form of which was up to the individual Mason. In Lodge, one could, at least in theory, see the working class shoulder to shoulder with the wealthy and aristocratic. In

---

108 As described in both Mackey's "Square" (Vol II, 708) and Mackenzie's "Square" (Vol. II, 690).

109 Cf. Mackey's "Rose Croix, Jewel of the" (Vol II, 635).

practice, this wasn't always the case, and elements of classism and racism, are discernable in Masonry's history. This was especially true in early Colonial Masonry, which often actively worked to keep lower social classes out of the lodge, generally the opposite of what was found in English Masonry during the same time.[110] After the near destruction of American Masonry in the early nineteenth century, due largely to the efforts of Evangelical anti-Masons, American Masonry moved away from that tendency. Even before this, American Masonry had moved toward the middle class, and members were proud of their middle-class backgrounds. It's possible that it was through the Lodge, Masonic or otherwise, that the middle class as an institution came into being.[111]

Members could, at least in theory, belong to nearly any religious denomination. The only universal religious requirement was the belief in a Supreme Being.[112] What that Being is, or how it is conceived, was no one's business but the Mason's. This was seen in practice, and in Victorian Europe and North America, one could, eventually, find Jews, Christians, Muslims, and Hindus working together in the same Lodge, all dedicated to the Great Architect of the Universe, however that figure might be understood.

This dedication to egalitarianism made sense in light of Masonry's teachings. The lesson on the symbol of the level, for instance, taught that all people were equal and should be approached, communicated with, and worked with, on that principle. These two elements, the at least theoretical blurring of class lines and the acceptance of religious differences were fairly groundbreaking, especially in a society where such differences could lead to the separation of the different parties in the social

---

110 See Bullock "The Appearance of SO Many Gentlemen" (50–81).

111 See Carnes 31–32.

112 Some Grand Lodges also require a belief in an immortal soul.

arena. The bringing up of such differences was quelled, in part, by the stipulation that neither politics nor religion could be discussed in an open Lodge.[113]

All of this was in alignment with Masonry's professed goals: to encourage personal and societal improvement, to foster friendship and community between all people, and the charitable relief to the distressed. Each of these were stressed in the rites of both Blue and Red Lodge Masonry.[114]

ESOTERICISM

Despite Masonry's social and personal goals, laudable as they might be, these alone did not greatly set it apart from other fraternities of this time, such as the International Order of Oddfellows and the Fraternal Order of Eagles, both of which exist today; or even Kiwanis and Jaycees, both of which were founded in the twentieth century. All of these taught and enforced various elements of morality and charity. From at least the 1700s, Masons tended to see Masonry as part of the *philosophia perennis*. Various "histories" of Masonry connected it to the druids, Pythagoreans, Hermetists and Hermeticists,[115] Knights Templar, and Rosicrucians, amongst others. There has long been a distinct occult element to Masonry, which was popularized in the 1700s and greatly expanded upon by the Victorians. Some

---

113 Among Lodges chartered from the UGLE, or Grand Lodges that came from the same tradition, such as those in the US. The Grand Orient de France didn't have the same sensibilities or restrictions as their English-derived counterparts.

114 Cf. Pike, 91, 536, 803.

115 The two terms are found in some academic writing to distinguish between the original writers and users of the Hermetic texts through the fourth century CE (Hermetists) and the later interpreters or critics of those texts from the Middle Ages and beyond (Hermeticists).

of these groups, from which Masonry may have been—but probably wasn't—derived, are important to understanding the history of Masonry and the occult organizations which sprung from it, so some discussion of them is necessary.

THE KNIGHTS TEMPLAR

Although the Pythagoreans are easily the oldest group with whom Freemasonry has been associated, the Knights Templar are those most closely associated with Masonic history. According to historians, the Templars were founded by nine French knights in 1118, after the first Crusade, for the purpose of protecting Christian pilgrims in the Holy Land. Under the patronage of the eventual saint Bernard of Clairvaux, this order of knights would be granted papal recognition and protection, and a Rule based on the Cistercian Order of Monks. It was at this point the knights officially became the *Pauperes commilitones Christi et Templi Salomonis,* the Poor Fellow Soldiers of Christ and of the Temple of Solomon, or more simply, the Knights Templar.[116]

According to some esoteric traditions, the Templars were not just a military order with monkish leanings. They were said to have connections with Gnosticism, Neoplatonism, Jewish and Muslim mysticism, and the Druze.[117] The work of the Templars was therefore not just the work of arms but of the spirit. They have been associated with the Holy Grail, alchemy, and various mystical practices.

After winning—and losing—several important battles during the Crusades, and having amassed both wealth and power, King Philippe IV, or Philippe le Bel as he was known, successfully conspired with Guillaume de Nogaret to suppress the Templars, presumably to seize their wealth. With the possibly coerced

---

116 See "Knights Templar" in Mackey's Encyclopedia, Vol I 542.
117 See Hogan 15, 23, 26–27, 29 38–39.

cooperation of the relatively weak Pope Clement V, the Templars in France were arrested on Friday the thirteenth, 1307, and officially suppressed by papal decree in 1312.[118] Grandmaster Jacques de Molay and a few hundred knights were burnt at the stake in 1314.

According to the traditions of some modern occult Templar orders, although officially suppressed, the Order did not end at this time. Many Templars fled to other European countries, where the suppression orders were not carried out. The most notable of these was Scotland, the presumed home of Freemasonry. The hidden Templars were said to have supported Robert the Bruce, soon to be King Robert I of Scotland, and to have been absorbed into the Order of Saint Andrew and later the Order of the Thistle,[119] though not everyone accepts this history.[120] They were also said to have moved into the stonemason's trade,[121] and through their influence, Operative Masonry became Speculative.

Whether or not any of this happened remains open to speculation, but the Templar connection was so important to Masonry that the two largest appellate bodies, the Scottish and York Rites, both had Templar degrees.[122] Of these, the York Rites are the most well-known and established as being Templar, with an entire system of Commandaries set up around them. The York Rite Templar degrees probably originated no earlier than the mid-to-late eighteenth century.[123]

---

118 See Mackey's History 256.

119 See Hogan 43.

120 See Mackey's History 258–259.

121 Ibid. 44.

122 Unlike the Scottish Rite degrees, to take the Templar York Rite degrees, depending on the Commandery, one must either be Christian or at least be willing to take a Christian oath.

123 See Evans 35–36.

The York Rite Templar rituals used a new method of initiation. While the Blue Lodge degrees were dramatic in nature, they appealed to the candidate's sense of reason to accomplish their work. The Templar degrees attempted to bypass the candidate's reason to access their moral character.[124] They used high drama to accomplish this, culminating in the candidate drinking from a skull.[125] The York Rite's popularity marked a renewed, or in the case of American Masonry, new, interest in the ancient mystery traditions.[126]

CHARACTER SKETCH: THE KNIGHT

By day, Henry Brougham is a bricklayer working in Liverpool. On every third Wednesday, Sir Henry Jonathan Thomas Brougham III is a Knight Companion of the Ordo Rubeus Crux Ansata, an ancient magical order whose lineage can be traced back to the temples of Hermopolis and through the rise and downfall of the Knights Templar. Also a Freemason, Sir Henry spends a great deal of his off time engaged with a number of charitable organizations for the relief of widows and orphans of those who died in industrial accidents.

Sir Henry is shown in the black cloak of the Order, which would show his degree and rank through the color of the lining of black, white, or red. These colors are purposefully connected to the three phases of the alchemical process. The long coat is not specifically connected to the Order's symbolism but does recall the frock coats worn in some Masonic Templar degrees. A cybernetic arm completes the steampunk look.

---

124 See Bullock 262–263, 270–272.

125 Ibid. 253–255.

126 Ibid. 266–268.

THE ROSE + CROIX

Perhaps the only other aspect of Masonry as popular as Templarism is Rosicrucianism. Rosicrucianism reached new heights of popularity in the late 1800s and early 1900s, both within and without Freemasonry. Most of what is known, or believed, about the Rosicrucians comes from the publication of the so-called Rosicrucian Manifestos: the *Fama Fraternitatis*, the *Confessio Fraternitatis*, and the *Chymical Wedding of Christian Rosenkretuz*, which were published between 1614 and 1616 in Kessel, Germany.

According to the *Fama*, the Rosicrucian Order was founded by one Father C. R. or C. R. C., identified in the third manifesto as Christian Rosenkreutz, sometime in the early fifteenth century. C. R. C. was said to have been born in 1378 and lived for 106 years. During his early life, C. R. C. traveled as a monk through Europe and the Near and Middle East in search of religious, philosophical, medical, and esoteric wisdom. After having learned all he could, he returned to Europe and founded the Rosicrucian Order or the Order of the Golden and Rosy Cross. In the Order, he distilled his vast knowledge and gathered like-minded individuals. After the first few generations of Rosicrucians died, the Order disappeared from the public, only to announce their reappearance through the manifestos. The *Fama* declared that the wise of Europe could join the Order. All they had to do was publicly announce their interest and a member of the Order would get in contact with them. So far as anyone can tell, no one was ever contacted.

The Rosicrucian Order as presented in the manifestos was an esoteric order, especially known for the practice of alchemy. According to a different tradition, the Rosicrucians predate the timeline in the manifestos. In this tradition, they came from Egypt before the eighth century CE and the Rosicrucian tradition was then brought to Europe in the ninth century. The Rosicrucian name was a rendering of the name of the Egyptian city from which it came, Ros Tou (now Giza), into Greek.[127] This same tradition says

---

127 Esoteric etymology can be…interesting.

there was a military branch of the Order, the *Ordre des Chevaliers Faydits de la Colombe du Paraclet*, roughly "the Holy Order of the Banished Knights of the Dove of the Paraclete." Hugh de Payens and Godfrey de Saint-Omar, two of the nine founding Templars, were initiates of this Order, and so the Rosicrucians and Templars were connected in an ancient lineage.[128]

In the Scottish Rite, the 15°–18°, or 17°–18°[129] were under the auspices of the Chapter of the Rose Croix. Each of these degrees was described at length in Albert Pike's *Morals and Dogma*, published in 1871, with the degrees possibly having been established around 1747.[130] The height of this Chapter, the Knight Rose Croix,[131] used the symbolism of suffering and redemption and, through this, the overcoming of evil by goodness. It taught "the unity, immutability and goodness of God, the immorality of the Soul; and the ultimate defeat and extinction of evil and wrong and sorrow, by a Redeemer or Messiah yet to come if he has not already appeared."[132]

While the Rose Croix degrees were important in their own right, there were some questions as to whether or not they had any kind of connection to the mystical Rosicrucians.[133] Like the Blue Lodge degrees, this was an allegorical and moral degree rather than one which taught theurgy or alchemy. There were, of course, esoteric interpretations of the degrees, potentially connecting them ideologically, if not historically, to pre-Masonic Rosicrucianism.[134] As such, a different Rosicrucian Masonically-related body was perhaps even more important: the Societas Rosicruciana (Soc. Ros.).

---

128 See Hogan 15–17. Cf. "Rosicrucianism" in Mackenzie 615–616.

129 This depends on jurisdiction. The former represents the Southern Jurisdiction of the United States, and the latter the Northern Jurisdiction. British forms of the Rite also vary on this.

130 See Makenzie under "Rose Croix, Prince of" (611).

131 Or Prince.

132 Pike 287.

133 See "Rosicrucianism" in Mackey 640.

134 Cf. Zeldis's "An Esoteric View of the Rose-Croix Degree."

The London branch of the Soc. Ros. was founded by Robert Wentworth Little around 1855. While not a Masonic appellate rite, one had to be a Master Mason,[135] as well as a Trinitarian Christian, to join. The Soc. Ros. had nine degrees, which would eventually be associated with the mystical Tree of Life of the Qabalah. Whereas the interests of Masonry were largely moral and philanthropic, those of the Soc. Ros. were decidedly esoteric, with a special focus on a Christianized form of Jewish mysticism. This interest, though, was largely theoretical in nature. They were not practicing magicians. The Soc. Ros. in England would eventually come under the leadership of Dr. William Wynn Westcott, who would help create one of the most notable magical orders of Victoriana, and arguably today as well, the Order of the Golden Dawn.

CHARACTER SKETCH:
THE ROSICRUCIAN

Ambrose Titus Saloman is a music teacher from Dayton, Ohio. Mr. Saloman's interest in the occult began later in life when his only child, Constanze Eliza, was cured of a rare disease by the local pharmacist, an alchemist by the name of Franklin Chan. Through this, Mr. Saloman discovered the Fellowship of the Rose + Croix of Abiengus, of which Brother Ambrose is a member of the VII°, an Adeptus Exemptus. The Fellowship focuses on the practical use of alchemy and optics and several members give lectures on theoretical or philosophical magic. The actual practice of magic is, of course, frowned upon as being fanciful, whereas alchemy is grounded in scientific principles. Brother Ambrose supplements his teaching income by selling alchemically produced tinctures at Mr. Chan's pharmacy. The price of which is always negotiable, no one is ever turned away due to poverty, and somehow the money always finds its way back into the community.

---

135 From a recognized malecraft Grand Lodge.

Brother Ambrose is dressed for Lodge in a traditional frock coat, waistcoat, and bowler hat. He wears a white collar embroidered with the symbols of his degree. Suspended from this is the rose cross his order takes its name from. Further symbols of authority are marked upon the scarlet sash about his waist. As the current Hierophant of his Lodge, Brother Ambrose holds the scepter of his position.

PRINCE HALL MASONRY

The above discussion focused primarily on Anglo-American malecraft Freemasonry, which is Masonry's most well-known form. More specifically, the above discussion focused largely on *White* Anglo-American Freemasonry. However, the history of Masonry is not just the history of a White, European institution. Masonry today exists all over the world. An important Black branch of Masonry appeared early in American Masonic history: Prince Hall Masonry.

Prince Hall was a man of contested lineage. He was of African descent and might have been born into slavery and freed in 1770. Or, he was possibly the son of a free African woman of French descent. Or maybe he was something else; there is no agreement on the subject. However, the subject of whether or not Hall was born into slavery is significant. The UGLE's constitution, beginning in 1847, allowed all free men, regardless of birth, to become Masons. The hallmarks followed in the US, until the early twentieth century, only allowed men who were born free to become Masons, excluding both those who had been enslaved and those who had been emancipated. Despite this, it appears Hall became a Mason in 1775.[136] This likely occurred in a military Lodge attached to General Thomas Gage's regiment and operated under the authority of the Grand Lodge of Ireland. Shortly after his initiation, Hall formed the first Black lodge,

---

136 See Révauger 9–11.

African Lodge no. 459, in Boston. This Lodge was granted a dispensation for its Black brothers to meet as Masons, and the Lodge was granted a charter from the Grand Lodge of England as early as 1784.[137] African Lodge's dispensation from the Grand Lodge of Ireland was problematic as it did not grant the authority to initiate new members. Hall attempted to join another Grand Lodge to get around this and was promised a charter by Joseph Warren, the Grand Master of the Grand Lodge of Massachusetts. However, Warren was killed in the Battle of Bunker Hill before granting the charter. Difficulties ensued, especially as Massachusetts hypocritically had two Grand Lodges but would not countenance a Black Grand Lodge, because only one Grand Lodge, which of course would be White, could exist in any territory. Hall turned to the Grand Lodge of England.[138] The warrant granted him by the UGLE still survives.

White Grand Lodges, for nearly two hundred years, have attempted to deny the regularity[139] of the Prince Hall lodges, often while simultaneously denying Black Americans entry into the Craft. The first Black Grand Lodge appeared between 1797 and 1807, presumably when African Lodge declared itself a Grand Lodge, governing other Prince Hall lodges in Massachusetts. This, in itself, was hardly unusual; many White Grand Lodges gave back their charters to the UGLE during

---

137 See Révauger 13–15.

138 Ibid. 15–16.

139 "Regular" in this context means one that conforms to the generally accepted principles of Freemasonry (or to those accepted by whichever Lodge or Grand Lodge you're talking about). An irregular Lodge is one that is considered by other Grand Lodges to not follow the hallmarks of the Craft, such as having a charter and being attached to a regular Grand Lodge. Arguably, American Grand Lodges that gave back their charters during the war and then declared themselves Grand Lodges afterward are irregular, though none are actually considered so.

the revolution and subsequently declared themselves Grand Lodges with no one batting an eye.

As other Prince Hall Lodges formed and failed to gain warrants from White Grand Lodges, they turned to African Lodge, even when those Lodges were not in Massachusetts. By 1887, all Prince Hall Grand Lodges proclaimed their autonomy, just as White Grand Lodges had.[140] Black Masons, much like women mediums involved in Spiritualism, used their positions, and the norms of White Masonry, especially the idea of brotherhood, to fight against the hypocrisy present in White Lodges that refused Black members.[141] Although today, men of any race can ostensibly become Masons in the United States, Prince Hall Masonry is still very active and still controversial. Today, forty-six historically White Grand Lodges, and the District of Columbia, recognize Prince Hall Masons as regular, leaving too many Grand Lodges, largely from former Confederate states, that do not.

FRENCH MASONRY

In Europe, and especially in France, Masonry took on other forms with different emphases, prohibitions, and kinds of members. The first Masonic lodge in France may have been established as early as the late 1600s by Irish soldiers under Charles II of England, and much of early French Masonry was under the auspices of the London Grand Lodge. A break with the UGLE would occur in 1877 when members who did not profess a belief in a Supreme Being were admitted. Some Lodges rejected this and formed the Grande Loge de France while others accepted it and formed the Grande Orient de France. The Grande Orient de France would also, at various times, admit women married to Masons with their own initiation rituals.

Unlike the English and American Grand Lodges, the Grand Orient exerted a great deal of control over the Lodges

---

140 Ibid. 20–26.

141 See Bullock 160.

it chartered. This included control over the bestowing of the Grand Orient's own seven degrees, but also all the degrees of the Ancient and Accepted Rite and the degrees of all other rites which had sworn obedience to the Grand Orient.[142] Due to the connections between the Grand Orient and the civil authority, rites not recognized by the Grand Orient were also illegal and were often shut down by the police.

Amongst the various rites of the Grand Orient was the Rite of Memphis and Misraim. Originally separate rites, the Rite of Misraim dated to at least the 1730s, though according to some, it did not appear until 1805, originating in Milan.[143] This rite, having ninety degrees, contained many esoteric elements, including references to alchemy, Cabbalah, and, of course, Egypt. According to the older tradition, this rite was popularized by the alchemist known as Cagliostro. By 1814, the Rite had entered France. The Rite of Misraim failed to gain recognition by the Grand Orient and, because of this, became illegal and eventually ceased to be practiced.[144]

In 1839, the Rite of Memphis was founded by two Frenchmen, with eventually ninety-two degrees of initiation. This rite was likely based on the older Rite of Misraim. Like its predecessor, the Rite of Memphis also failed to gain recognition by the Grand Orient, and in 1852, its Lodges were closed by the civil authorities. However, in 1862, after another attempt at recognition by one of its founders, Jacques-Étienne Marconis de Nègre, the Rite was recognized. In achieving this, however, Marconis de Nègre lost all control of it. By the time of Queen Victoria, the Rite had been stripped of many of its higher degrees because the Grand Orient only recognized the thirty-three degrees of the Ancient and Accepted Rite.[145] By 1889, the Rites of Memphis and of Misraim had been fused by General Giuseppe Garibaldi, and by

---

142 See "Grand Orient" in Mackenzie 421.

143 Ibid. "Misraim, Rite of" (487).

144 Ibid.

145 Ibid. Memphis, Rite of," 480–481.

this time, the Rite of Memphis, though stripped of its glory in Lodges connected to the Grand Orient, had become popular as a form of "clandestine" or irregular Masonry outside of France. Garibaldi was succeeded by Theodor Reuss, the founder of the quasi-Masonic Ordo Templi Orientis, which was eventually connected to the Edwardian magician Aleister Crowley.

CO-MASONRY

Although the Grand Orient admitted women married to Masons, their initiation rites were distinct from those of their husbands. However, in the nineteenth century, Le Droit Humain, a Co-Masonic Order, accepted both women and men equally. Its founders were Maria Deraismes, a journalist and women's rights advocate, and Dr. Georges Martin, a senator and Grand Councilor for the Department of the Seine. Deraismes was initiated in 1882 in a small town outside of Paris. In 1894, Deraismes and Martin founded the first Co-Masonic Lodge in Paris and, from this, la Grande Loge symbolique écossaise.[146] Today, Le Droit Humain is recognized by the Grand Orient of France. While Le Droit Humain, as well as its offshoot, the Honorable Order of Universal Co-Masonry, recognized the United Grand Lodge of England and all the malecraft Grand Lodges of the United States, neither the UGLE nor the US Grand Lodges recognized Le Droit Humain. Le Droit Humain was never officially an occult order but had members with great interests in the subject, the most well-known being Annie Besant and C. W. Leadbeater, both of whom were prominent Theosophists. Both would also rise to the 33°, the highest degree of that Order, and Besant would become the Order's Most Puissant Grand Commander.

---

146 Le Droit Humain, "Origins and History of the American Federation," https://www.freemasonryformenandwomen.org/origins.html.

Besant was engaged in a number of social and esoteric endeavors. A member of the London School Board, having run as a Marxist, the Illustrious Brother Besant was president of the Indian National Congress in 1917 and founded the London branch of Le Droit Humain in 1902. Well-educated, Besant was active in the women's rights movement, both in England and India, and worked toward improving women's work conditions and pay. She was involved in the London matchgirls' strike in 1888 as well as Bloody Sunday. She was once arrested while working toward getting women the right to birth control.

Besant was introduced to Theosophy through Blavatsky's *The Secret Doctrine* in 1889 at the age of forty-one and became president of the Theosophical Society in 1907, which was then headquartered in Adyar, Madras. It was through the TS that she became interested in and then involved with India and its efforts to gain independence from England. Besant made India her home in 1893. Rather the opposite of the Colonel, however, she also worked to limit the influence of Buddhism in India and attempted to steer Indians toward Hinduism instead.

Well-known in occult circles, Besant was equally well-known as a social reformer and activist, both in England and India. A proponent of education for women, she helped establish the Central Hindu College in Varanasi and assisted in the founding of the Hyderabad National Collegiate Board in Mumbai.[147]

---

147 See "Annie Besant" at www.varanasi.org.in/annie-besant.

CHAPTER FIVE

LOW MAGIC IN THE
AGE OF STEAM

While the focus of this book is on Victorian high magic and the traditions that led to and informed it, we cannot ignore ceremonial magic's more rustic cousins. Although alternative spiritualities grounded in the Christianity of Victoria's time were perhaps the most common, they were not the only movements toward esotericism. Many, such as Olcott, would turn to the East and engage in traditional forms of Buddhism, Hinduism, or Daoism. Some would turn to Islam and the Sufis. But there were other options. People also turned their eyes toward what they perceived to be their own distant pasts, and especially toward the religions of the Scandinavians and Celts. Others looked to the cunning traditions stemming from the British countryside. In America, many people of color—especially the formerly enslaved—turned, or returned, to their religious traditions, both African Traditional and diaspora religions such as Vodou, Santería, and Candomblé once Christianity was no longer forced upon them.

THE FAIRY-FAITH

While fraternal organizations and mystery schools flourished during the latter part of the nineteenth century, not all magicians focused solely on high magic. W. B. Yeats, Irish poet, playwright, and Nobel Prize winner for literature, had a deep interest in pre-Christian[148] Celtic religion and fairy lore. To this end, he produced a number of books on Irish mythology and fairy tradition, including *Fairy and Folk Tales of the Irish Peasantry* and *The Celtic Twilight,* as well as numerous poems and plays based on the subject. He also worked with S. L. MacGregor Mathers, one of the founders of the Golden Dawn, on a Celti-form version of ceremonial magic. This would have employed the names of various Celtic deities rather than Hebrew divine names. Numerous other books on the mythologies of the various Celtic peoples, as well as books on fairy-faith, also appeared at this time. One of the most popular books, *The Secret Commonwealth of Elves, Fauns, and Fairies,* by Robert Kirk, was originally published in the seventeenth century and regained popularity in the late nineteenth—and is still available today.

The Victorians approached Celtic lore in a number of different ways. Walter Yeeling Evans-Wentz,[149] for instance, examined the phenomenon of fairy sightings and lore from something of an academic perspective.[150] Evans-Wentz proposed a number of theories, ranging from hidden races of dwarves to disembodied spirits. There is difficulty here, however. English scholars typically approached anything Celtic from the perspective of the Empire

---

148 Or what he believed was pre-Christian. Celtic studies as a scholarly discipline did not exist at this time and the information that was propagated by contemporary scholars and other inquirers were often mistaken, filled with misinterpretations, and sometimes just made up.

149 See The Fairy-Faith in Celtic Countries by Evans-Wentz.

150 Keep in mind that nineteenth-century's and twenty-first-century's academic standards are almost entirely different.

and as colonizers. Relatively little was known about the subject as well, so much of the information available at the time was suspect at best.

Others, such as Yeats, seemed to be more interested in working with the Celtic fairies and gods. Yeats's work, what little is known of it, appears to focus on the Tuatha Dé Danann, who are generally understood by practitioners to be the ancient Irish gods. Yeats, however, was also well-versed in Irish mythology in general and included the Irish epic cycles in his work. The tragic hero Cú Chulainn figures in several of his poems and plays.

By applying these figures to the Qabalistic Tree of Life, as in his Golden Dawn work, Yeats would have been able to access these deities and spirits through ritual, meditation, and the use of sacred symbols. For instance, Yeats recounted an encounter with a seer who, having been given "a certain old Irish symbol," had a vision of Brigit, an Irish goddess.[151] While an interest in these subjects was present in Victorian society, we do not see a widespread or systematic attempt to reconstruct such beliefs and practices for modern use such as we do today.

CHARACTER SKETCHES: THE FAE

There is nothing that requires one's steamsona to be human. While there is nothing particularly different in how someone of the fairy-faith might dress and adorn themselves in comparison to anyone else, the fae are another matter entirely. Traditional lore surrounding the fae is often dark, and the fae can be beautiful or hideous, neither of which necessarily belays their personalities. Those who can use glamour, a magic to change one's appearance, can, and do, appear as they want; their visage depends on the circumstances of their purpose, reception, and treatment, their true demeanor not appearing until it is too late to do anything about it.

---

151 See Yeats's "Ideas of Good and Evil."

The fairies with butterfly wings and little dresses are largely of Victorian and Edwardian invention. This image of fairies was popularized by the Cottingley fairies phenomenon. These appeared in photographs taken by the young Elsie Wright and Frances Griffiths in the early twentieth century. While the cousins eventually admitted the pictures were faked,[152] the image of this kind of fairy has remained in popular imagination. But, as we learned in Jim Henson's 1986 film *Labyrinth*, just because they're pretty doesn't mean they don't bite. This fairy is dressed for the beach in a Victorian swimsuit. She hovers about as she enjoys her afternoon tea.

Redcaps, sometimes called powries or dunters, are just one kind of fae found in traditional lore, and they are on the hideous side of the fae aesthetics spectrum. The most well-known is Robin Redcap, the familiar of the sorcerer Lord William de Soulis, a man so evil legend says that once he was finally captured, the locals wrapped him in lead and boiled him alive. To call redcaps murderous is inaccurate only in that "murderous" isn't a strong enough term. The diminutive creatures are called redcaps because of the cap they wear, which is soaked in the blood of their meals—preferably humans. Tradition says that if the blood on their cap dried completely, the redcap would die.

This fellow is wearing an oversized coachman's coat, taken off one of his meals. Pointed ears poke out from his red cap and he holds a Lochaber axe. The mechanical arm is composed of brass and is held together with fae magic. Tradition also had them with various other weapons and tools, such as knives and daggers. Robin Redcap was described as wielding a pike.

The fae come in any number of shapes and sizes. Some wear particular dress, such as all red or red and green, and some are said to wear clothing in the style of their surrounding human culture. Traditional fairy lore generally does not depict them with wings,

152 In 1983, in a magazine called The Unexplained.

and those who can fly just do so without any obvious means. Wings, of course, are now part of the modern, popular image of fairies. There isn't really a rule here, and in many instances, what will set you apart from everyone else is the accouterments, makeup, and prosthetics that you might use to make you look less human and more something else.

DRUIDRY

For as long as there has been recorded religious history, humans have looked to past religions and practices to inform their present. This is not necessarily because their present practices or beliefs are lacking; it is simply a human thing to do. We can see this in Christianity and Judaism but also in the Romans, who looked back to the Greeks and Egyptians for inspiration, and even occasionally to Judaism. That various British peoples would look to the Celts should come as no surprise.

In the seventeenth and eighteenth centuries, England and Wales[153] saw a renewed interest in the Celtic peoples and, especially, their priests and wizards, the druids. Although bardic traditions survived in Wales, Ireland, and Scotland until the seventeenth century, not only had bardcraft become largely Christianized, but other elements of the Celtic magical and priestly practice were often not retained, such as the work of the ovates, or diviners, and druids "proper."[154] These other elements would interest those who would revive, create, and/or recreate druidic traditions.

Writers such as Irish-born and Scottish-educated John Toland and William Stukeley lauded the ancient druids for their wis-dom and learning[155] and would even create a modern Druidic Order,[156]

---

153 This never really died in Scotland and Ireland, though it may have occasionally been outlawed as being, well, Celtic.

154 See Carr-Gomm 10–11.

155 See Hutton's Triumph 9.

156 To avoid confusion, the ancient druids and modern Druidic Orders are distinguished by the use of the capitalization of the latter.

and either lampoon the Anglican Church or offer Druidic teachings to Christians.[157] Regardless of their anti-Anglican, or pro-druidic, bent, modern Druid groups began springing up all over Britain. This posed some difficulties, given the limited amount of accurate information on the Celts in general, and the druids in specific, that was available at that time, or even until the middle of the twentieth century. These modern Druids used anything available to them to create a druidic practice and/or spirituality.[158] While such (re)invented spiritualities often had little to do with actual ancient Celtic beliefs, they were often on the leading edge of what today we might call Celtic Studies.[159]

The early druidic revival often focused on pantheism rather than polytheism, seeing the world itself as being divine. There was also a deep ecological concern connected to the eighteenth-century druidic revival, which continues in many of today's Druidic organizations. These modern Druids gave themselves ancient lineages, sometimes tracing themselves back as far as Noah.[160] As odd as this might seem, the idea did not originate with the eighteenth-century Druids, having its source in Irish mythology. The *Lebor Gabála Érenn*, or *The Book of the Taking of Ireland*, written down by Christian monks sometime before the mid-twelfth century, traces the founder of the Gaels back to the children and grandchildren of Noah.[161] The connection, though likely of Christian invention,[162] gave the modern Druids the legitimacy only an ancient lineage seems to provide.

Although John Aubrey possibly began the druid revival with the founding of Mount Haemus Grove in 1694, it was Toland

---

157 See John Michael Greer.

158 As we'll see, not all druidic organizations were, or are, religious or spiritual in nature.

159 See Greer's "Revival."

160 See Hutton's Triumph 59 and Greer's "Revival."

161 See §14–15 of Lebor Gabála Érenn.

162 This was sometimes necessary to give a reason for the survival of the story. Unmitigated paganism wouldn't have been allowed to survive.

who, in 1717, brought together a number of small druidic groups, or groves, to form the Universal Bond, more commonly referred to as the Druid Order, with Toland as its first Chosen Chief.[163] According to its traditions, the Druid Order existed along a chain of continuous Chosen Chiefs, from antiquity to the present time.[164] Stemming from the Druid Order was the Ancient Order of Druids, founded in London in 1781. This order, in line with the numerous clubs popular at that time, used druidic language for the purpose of social welfare and improvement. It came to America in 1830. In the case of both orders, the local groups within them functioned similarly to Masonic Lodges, and often for the same kind of purposes, just with different symbol sets and rituals.

While some, such as Toland, saw their orders as religious movements, others did not, as many of their members were practicing Christians. This use of pre-Christian Celtic religious symbolism, but not necessarily the practice of pre-Christian Celtic religion, can be seen in other druidic groups from this time. Many of the Welsh *eisteddfodau*, bardic festivals, used druidic language and even revived and popularized Welsh bardcraft.

These Druidic Orders celebrated what they believed were ancient Celtic holidays, such as the solstices and equinoxes, as well as the "cross-quarter" holidays, such as Samhain or Beltainne.[165] The orders also had rituals of initiation and, much like the Masons, degree systems. Their courses of study included Celtic, especially Welsh and Irish, mythology, history, bardcraft,

---

163 See Hutton's Blood and Mistletoe 125.

164 Nichols 98–99. The tradition is questionable. Ross Nichols, the founder of the Order of Bards, Ovates & Druids, was a member of the Ancient Druid Order (OBOD), which was an offshoot of this older Order, and which ceased to function for a brief period of time until the foundation of OBOD.

165 There is little evidence for Celtic peoples having used the equinoxes and solstices for religious celebration. Samhain, Beltainne, Lughnasadh, and Imbolc, or their Welsh and Continental equivalents, were the actual times of celebration.

magic, astrology, and divination with the Ogham alphabet. Though some can be found as early as the 1860s, much of the magical practice in the various Druidic Orders was not fully realized until the twentieth century. There was also significant Masonic influence.[166] Toland was a member of the Masonic-like, panentheistically-inclined Knights of Jubilation, and his successor, Stuckley, was a Freemason.[167]

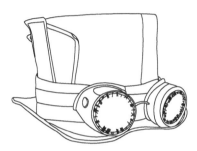

Early English Druidry was largely fraternal, even club-like, with a heavily romanticized view of the Celts. By the late eighteenth century, we began to see different forms of Druidry. Welsh Druidry had a nationalistic focus largely absent from the English orders, with its examinations for different bardic ranks given entirely in Welsh.[168] This was seen distinctly in the druidic revival created by the Welsh druidic bard, Edward James, better known by his bardic name, Iolo Morganwg. Morganwg founded the Gorsedd Beirdd Ynys Prydain in 1792 to promote Welsh poetry and music, and the *gorseddau,* ceremonial ritual circles, still exist.

According to Morganwg, the ancient druids were bardic in nature and had four divisions: *bardd braint, derwydd, ovydd,* and *awenyddion.* The *awenyddion* were apprentices who would

---

166 Cf. Hutton's Blood and Mistletoe, 342–343, 351–352.

167 See Strickland.

168 Nichols 116. Queen Elizabeth II was initiated into one such Order. She was later expelled because she had never learned to speak Welsh.

eventually enter one of the other bardic classes. The *bardd braint*, or "true bard," was the heart of the order; both *derwydd* and *ovydd* were also bards, but ones who focused on things other than bardcraft alone. A *derwydd*, or druid, was not of a higher grade than a bard but instead was a bard who focused on religion and education. The *ovyddu* were the vates or ovates of English Druidry. Rather than focusing on divination, this was an honorary position granted to those who gained renown in science or literature. The different types of bards were distinguished by the color of their robes: blue, white, or green.[169]

Morganwg's writings also included the *Barddas*, which he purported to be the genuine teachings of the ancient Welsh bards. The *Barddas* included poetry as well as "triads" or wisdom sayings, based on authentically ancient triadic sayings. The *Barddas* also included a theological section with an esoteric cosmology and alphabets that had divinatory use.[170] However, most of the mystical elements in Welsh bardic Druidry were in the rituals rather than the overall *eisteddfodau*, or bardic competitive celebrations.[171]

Other Druidic Orders in the United Kingdom also existed, such as the Triple Order of Brittany, formed in 1899, and the Bards of Cornwall in 1928. Arthurian literature was also popular during this time, especially in Brittany, which has connections to Cornwall and Wales. The Triple Order, beginning with the Gorsedd Breizh, and continuing Welsh patterns of celebration, was authorized by the Welsh Archdruid Hwfo Mon. Due to later ties of friendship between the Order of Brittany and English druids, the Welsh *gorseddau* ceased to have relations with the former. Both the Cornish and Breton druidic orders were, like the Welsh, founded largely to be nationalistic in nature. The

---

169 See Hutton's Blood and Mistletoe 157.
170 Both volumes of the Barddas are available online. See bibliography.
171 See Nichols 116.

French order, however, worked along different lines. The Collège bardique des Gaules's most prominent member was Phileas Lebesque. Lebesque was a philosopher, humanist, storyteller, and romantic who rejected the skepticism of the period. These, along with elements of the French occult renaissance from the 1700s, were found in the Collège and its four grades of *bardes*,[172] *ouates*,[173] *eubages*,[174] and *druides*.[175]

CHARACTER SKETCH: THE DRUID

Dame Eiluned is an *ovydd* of the Henge of the Broken Gear. While members of the Henge partake of elements of the traditional Welsh *gorseddau*, especially the bardic competitions, their primary focus is environmentalism. While some are proclaiming the wonders of new, phlogiston-powered technologies, Dame Eiluned divines the desolated future they portend when, not if, they are misused. As a baronetess, Dame Eiluned uses her influence and wealth to support charities dedicated to environmentalism. As an *ovydd*, she uses her second sight to guide both those charities and the magic of the Henge's *derwydds* toward the same ends.

---

172 Generally related to poetry, songcraft, and storytelling.

173 This word is found in Ceasar's description of the ancient Gallic druids. The vates or ovates performed sacrifices and read omens from them. Today, the degree is more associated with divination than animal sacrifice. Carr-Gomm 10.

174 Although Toland believed the word came from the Irish eu faigh, "good poet," (Toland 268) it is more likely to come from the Greek ouateis, from whence the terms vate and ovate, are derived (ibid.). See also Carr-Gomm 10.

175 This degree is often related to magic and, in some very modern instances, the clergy.

Dame Eiluned wears a deeply hooded long coat, which keeps in the style of the period while recalling the colored robes of the various druidic orders. The sickle, according to Roman writers, was used by the druids to harvest sacred mistletoe from oak trees. It could, of course, be used for sacrifices, although they were traditionally said to have been made of gold, and thus not overly great for keeping an edge. Added to any druidic-inspired look could be the runes from the *Barddas* or the Irish Ogham writing, which was generally used on monuments and markers but is today used for talismanic and divinatory purposes as well.

A VIKING REVIVAL

Historically, the English viewed the Vikings in a decidedly negative light. English heritage was tied to Germanic heritage and history through the Saxons, and so there existed a tension between an interest in that history and a dislike of the "barbaric" Vikings. Some of this began to change in the eighteenth century when Viking-era texts started to circulate amongst a small group of interested parties, and more so in the eighteenth century when Norse mythology began to become popular. However, it was during the nineteenth century, with the rise of German Romanticism,[176] and especially during the Victorian era, that old Norse culture became popular among the English.[177]

Linguists began studying old Germanic languages and found the roots of local idioms in such. Archeologists opened cairns. Runic inscriptions were translated. What was found was a rich culture and a highly developed religion.[178] Precisely the opposite of how the pre-Christian Northern Europeans had been viewed. The Romantics engaged in this endeavor

---

176 See Von Schnurbein 17.

177 See Wawn.

178 Ibid.

developed ideas of holistic unity with nature and its expression through mythology.[179]

In Germany, a call to "Germanize" religion occurred in the 1870s, led by scholars such as the orientalist Paul de Lagarde. De Lagarde rejected both Catholicism and Protestantism, the primary forms of German Christianity, and saw a need to counter the materialism of the new German empire with a much-needed, authentically German, spirituality. Notions of Germanizing Christianity were taken up by others by the end of the nineteenth century, which quickly included racist and anti-Semitic elements drawn from French—and the Theosophical Society's—racial theory.

The Icelandic Sagas were then introduced into this intellectual milieu.[180] Although written down by Christian monks in the twelfth and thirteenth centuries, at the time they were considered authentic oral traditions passed down untouched by heathen forebearers.

English interests in the subject went in different directions. Also, unlike within some modern Druidic organizations, there were no class distinctions or territorial boundaries in the English, and sometimes Anglo-American, interest in Germanic religion. This spread even to Queen Victoria's courts, where rumors of her being a descendant of Odin, the chief of the Germanic gods, and her entire family from a Viking king. By the beginning of the twentieth century, pre-Christian Norse and Icelandic culture had become so popular that adhering to "Viking values" was a prevalent trend.[181] However, the growth

---

179 Von Schnurbein 17. In Germany, toward 1910, elements German Romanticism would be taken to radical German völkisch nationalism, which included significant elements of racism and anti-Semitism. Hopefully it's needless to say that this should be avoided in your persona.

180 Ibid. 29–30.

181 See Wawn.

of such interests into lasting orders or religious groups did not occur until late the twentieth century. Instead, these traditions seem to have nested closer to home, having become enculturated, rather than separated in the form of mystery traditions as seen amongst the druids.

CUNNING FOLK

Cunning folk were, and are, practitioners of magic once common to rural England. They professed to cure the sick, unbewitch the beleaguered, bring love, find robbers, and cast all manner of charms. The term "cunning" is derived from the Anglo-Saxon *cunnan,* "to know," and so cunning folk were those who knew more than those around them. This knowledge was gained through supernatural means, an innate heredity ability, or simply because they happened to be literate.[182] They were wizards and conjurors, wise-folk and witches, practitioners of magic and legerdemain.

Cunning folk made a living off their Craft and were interested in the application of magic to deal with common, everyday problems. They were a common part of English society between the seventeenth and nineteenth centuries, though they can be found earlier than this. Cunning traditions continue today and were influential on the twentieth-century Traditional Witchcraft revival. Their services included fortune telling, midwifery, curing the sick, and anti-witchcraft magic. They could find thieves and treasure and even kill suspected witches by magical means. No job was too small to take and, outside of raising the dead, no job too big,[183] as one's reputation could grow by small and large jobs alike.

Cunning folk typically, though not always, came from rural parts of the country, and often from lower economic classes. However, many cunning folk were both literate and wealthy enough to afford

---

182 See Davis's Popular Magic.
183 See Davis 93–94.

a number of books. These included books of high or ceremonial magic, the knowledge of which was often spread by cunning folk. They often owned other books to show off to their clients, the bigger, fancier, and older the better.[184] Cunning folk also had a book of practice, which contained spells, charms, and rituals they found useful. Such books might contain elements of not only folk magical traditions but excerpts from grimoires and related texts[185] and served as a model for Wicca's Book of Shadows, which contains the rituals and personal notes of the witch who wrote it.

Unlike much of the rest of the traditions discussed in this chapter, cunning folk were typically Christians and had no qualms with employing saints in their magic, a practice also common to Hoodoo or root working. For instance, a charm against toothaches recalled Saint Peter being cured by Christ. Other charms employed the names of the "Father, Son, and Holy Ghost."[186] The grimoire tradition from which cunning folk drew was also largely Christian in nature.

WHAT ABOUT WICCA?

Many readers might be familiar with the Witchcraft religion called Wicca. The history of the religion has been researched and written about by many people, the most important of whom being Professor Ronald Hutton and Philip Heselton. What we find concerning Wicca is that it is a modern, syncretic tradition, likely developed in the 1940s[187] and popularized in the 1960s. While Wicca contains elements of English, Germanic, and Celtic folk traditions, its development also relied heavily on Masonry and Co-Masonry, the Ordo Templi Orientis, modern Druidry, and ceremonial magic from the Order of the Golden Dawn.

---

184 Ibid. 119.

185 See Davis 133 and also Rankine's Grimoire.

186 See Pennick 126.

187 Arguably, Wicca would be dieselpunk.

Does that mean your steampunk persona can't be influenced by Wicca or Wiccan aesthetics? Absolutely not. While a modern religion, Wicca's syncretism is entirely in keeping with Victoriana. More importantly, steampunk is a form of fantasy. Our restrictions are not on the time something occurred—or if it occurred at all—but on how we are going to engage with it in a respectful way. Wicca is, after all, a living religion, and should be respected as such in the development of our personae.

CHARACTER SKETCH: THE CUNNING WOMAN

Arabella Bennet is a witch and cunning woman from the coastal town of New Swanage, Maryland. Known especially for healing and talismanry, Bella rarely turns away someone truly in need. Often bartering her services, she is known for miles around as the wise woman who will get you out of the troubles no respectable doctor, or magician, will touch. Need a charm to drive away unwanted suitors or a spell to ward off the evil eye? Turned into a newt? Bella will help you get better. Described by her friends as a book nerd, Bella's personal library is both impressive and accessible. For a price.

A Victorian-inspired dress clothes the character. This is complemented by a leather collar, harness, and reagent bags. The bags are marked with the Theban script, which was used as early as the late sixteenth century. Rather than representing

some ancient language, Theban is simply a different alphabet applied to the common Roman alphabet. It has been used since at least the nineteenth century for occult purposes. It can be seen on talismans and some have written their entire Book of Shadows in it. A steampunk take on the pointed witch's hat finishes off the look.

BEYOND THE PALE: HAITIAN VODOU

For both its survival and, perhaps more importantly, its relevance, steampunk must transcend its White, English-speaking, Anglo-American origins. English speakers were hardly the only people influenced by Victoriana—including the rejection of it—nor were they the only ones with interests in the occult. It is beyond the scope of this book and my linguistic ability to engage in what is going on in the majority of Europe, let alone outside of Europe, regarding the occultisms of that era, although I look forward to reading books on those subjects. In an attempt to move in this direction, however, we will look at esotericism and religion in Haiti—specifically, Vodou, or what its practitioners may call "serving the *lwa*" or "following the *lwa*."

From the sixteenth to the early seventeenth centuries, the island of what is now the Republic of Haiti was ruled by the Spanish after their consequent of the native Taíno peoples. After the seventeenth century, and until 1804, Haiti, renamed Saint-Domingue, was ruled by the French. On January 1, 1804, Jean-Jacques Dessalines, who was part dictator, part national hero, and speaking in Creole rather than French, declared Haitian independence. He began a successful revolution against the French, the savagery of which might be compared to Robespierre's Reign of Terror.[188]

The majority of Haitians were then Creole-speaking laborers. A handful of Haitian scholars tried to write about Haiti in a way

---

188 Cf. Dayan 4.

 89

that presented it in a good light to a White audience while still identifying with their own Haitianness. Overall, there was an attempt to demonstrate to a White world that Blackness did not equate to barbarianism.[189] In fact, many writers, especially during and after the revolution, placed the savagery of the revolution firmly on the shoulders of the French; in order to overthrow imperialism, the tactics of the imperialists had to be used.[190] The extent to which this was playing upon White, French, attitudes for Haitian advantage is questionable.

Vodou rituals are frequently considered to have been at least partially behind the success of the revolution. Folk leaders such as Macandal, a *papalwa* or high priest, arose to lead the people. Ritual dances to the *lwa* were held before raids and attacks against the French, and although Macandal was killed in 1758, his vision of not only a free people, but a people who could return to Africa, did not die with him. Following Macandal was Boukman, who, according to tradition, oversaw a Vodou ritual in the Bois Caïman forest in 1791.[191]

The earliest reference to Vodou in Haiti is in 1814, in a book that described the Bois Caïman ceremony. Although this ritual may have been invented by those who disdained native Haitian culture and religion, many Haitians turned to it as a foundation for their national identity.[192] Following the ceremony, Boukman led the most devastating attack on the French colony to that point.[193]

Just as Haitian identity was for many formed around Vodou, Vodou and its *lwa* were formed around the development of Haitian identity. It, and they, took on characteristics of the enslaved and formerly enslaved, but also those of the enslavers.[194]

---

189 Cf. Dayan 9.

190 Ibid. 4.

191 See DesMangles 33–34.

192 See Dayan 29.

193 See DesMangles 34.

194 See Dayan 30–31.

The *lwa* are beings that defy convenient placement into European spiritual hierarchies. They are *Mystères* or *Invisibles* and act as intermediaries between humanity and Bondye, the unknowable Supreme Creator. Some of this is seen in the deification of Dessalines as Ogou Desalin, a *lwa krèyol,* a Creole spirit who walked with African Ogou, the gods of war and politics, in Haiti. Not all the *lwa* in Haitian Vodou originated in Africa, however. Many, especially those invoked today, were products of, and responses to, French slavery.[195] It was not, however, the presence of a White oppressor which caused a need for Haitians to turn to the *lwa.* The need was always there. The revolution did not create, or recreate, Vodou, it simply brought it out into the open.

Vodou itself, especially before White people became interested in its practices, was heavily connected to the land and the blood of those who practiced it. The *demanbre,* a sacred plot of land, was central to spiritual identity and could not be sold or divided. Those who remembered their heritage and history, and the *lwa,* were reclaimed by the ancestors and lived on after death. Those who forgot their heritage might be oppressed by the *lwa.*[196]

The *lwa* represented one of the most complex elements of Vodou. There were numerous *lwa,* some of whom, such as Baron Samedi and Papa Legba, have even found their way into American pop culture. Not only were there many *lwa,* but there were also ancestors who could act as intermediaries between individuals and the *lwa* and had their own personal, often familial, concerns. As spiritual intermediaries between humanity and the Supreme Creator, the *lwa* took on many forms and did not necessarily represent a set number of such beings. Not all *lwa* got along with one another either, and their services could be interrupted by the uninvited presence of another *lwa.*[197] Like the *lwa,* their sects and initiated practitioners also rivaled

---

195 See Dayan 30, 36.

196 Ibid. 33.

197 Ibid. 84.

one another. Further complicating matters, there was a strong tradition of syncretism connecting the *lwa* with Roman Catholic saints, which only became stronger after 1860.

The initiated priests (*houngans*) and priestesses (*mambos*) acted to do good and protect others using Vodou, and might also have harmed, or even killed, others using the same. A *houngan* or *mambo* could be distinguished from either an initiated or noninitiated practitioner by their use of an *asson*, a rattle made from a *calabasse* tree. There are also the *bokor*, sorcerers for hire. Vodou became an official religion in Haiti in the twentieth century. Before then, its practice was punishable by law, and Vodouists formed secret societies to practice and propagate their religion.

There were a number of common Vodouist beliefs. First was the belief in the Supreme Creator, called *Bondye*, "Good God," or *Gran Met*, "Great Master." Bondye created the *lwa* as well as the ancestors and dead to help Vodouists in resolving their various problems. The *lwa* could be accessed through services and could help with matters of love, financial issues, protection, magic, possession, and prophecy. People were called to serve the *lwa* in different ways, some of which involved initiation and others not, and everyone was considered to have, or be attached to, at least one *lwa*, if not more.[198]

Vodou rites often took the form of ritualized singing and dancing, which sometimes appeared to be out of control. During these rituals, the *houngan* or *mambo* would draw the *vévé* of the *lwa* involved. This was like a ritual diagram of the cosmos which encapsulated a myth or myths concerning the *lwa* involved. The symbols of multiple *lwa* may be drawn in any given *vévé*, and the position of the symbol has cosmological significance.[199] Like Masonry and many traditions of ritual magic, Vodou is an initiatory tradition. However, unlike those, Vodou is much like Wicca, as it was and is a religion, not just a set of esoteric practices.

---

198 See "Haitian Vodou Beliefs."
199 See DesMangles 105–107.

CHARACTER SKETCH:
DO NOT EXPAND THE EMPIRE

Unless you are a person of color, affecting elements from Vodou into a steamsona, even if not taking something from Vodou itself, in a non-imperialist, nonracist manner is difficult, because such attitudes are systemically ingrained into White society. There are White practitioners of Vodou, and if you are one of those people, then go ahead, as you will know how to do so respectfully. Otherwise, I do not recommend it.

Then why include it? Because steampunk isn't just for and about White people. This is in no way to say that people of color should limit their esoteric steamsonas to Vodou or African-derived forms of esotericism or spirituality. Western esotericism exports itself everywhere. Simply put, there is more than just a European aesthetic in the world, and those should be part of steampunk too. But very often, unlike European cultures, they don't export themselves, and so should not simply be taken.

WHAT ABOUT MAGIC?

As can be seen, with the notable exception of cunning folk and the African-diaspora religions, we do not find much by way of magical practice amongst the Victorian circles, heaths, and groves. Although often drawing from older practices, most modern Pagan magical practice only begins well into the twentieth century, although some of the German rune magic does start in the late 1800s. What does this mean for your steampunk persona? As above, relatively little.

Just because we do not find strong evidence for a Victorian Pagan magical practice does not mean such practices cannot be incorporated into your steamsona. Nothing prevents you from having a steampunk *seiðrwoman*, or a druid diviner using runes or Ogham staves engraved on brass or a walking stick. Steampunk elements can be easily fused into aesthetics derived from such peoples and practices.

To do this, it is beneficial to research what modern Paganisms are doing. On this, I recommend looking not only at the practices themselves but also at how those practices developed. Especially useful in this are the works of Ross Nichols, founder of the largest druid order in the world, and Gerald Gardner, founder, or at least public transmitter, of Wicca. Modern Pagan religions also frequently have a strong material culture to look into as well. For instance, robes and amulets, which are readily available to purchase from practitioner-makers, can be brought into your steamsona's outfits, often with only minor modifications.

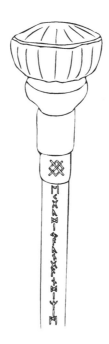

CHAPTER SIX

HIGH MAGIC IN THE AGE OF STEAM

The reorientation of the Theosophical Society from West to East left a vacuum. Blavatsky proclaimed that Westerners were not spiritually advanced enough to learn, let alone practice, magic. Until then, students of Qabalah, alchemy, Rosicrucianism, and other related traditions had a place to not only gather and talk but also practice their arts. This was now forbidden, and the Theosophical Society ceased teaching its form of "white magic," though some psychic skills were still taught. Even though many such enthusiasts were also Masons, Freemasonry had, by the nineteenth century, largely distanced itself from these traditions and was not, after all, a place for practicing magicians to perform their art. One of the first organizations to attempt to fill this gap was the Hermetic Brotherhood of Luxor (H.B. of L.), traditionally said to have been founded in 1870 by Max Theon.

THE HERMETIC
BROTHERHOOD OF LUXOR

The Hermetic Brotherhood of Luxor was an order of practical magic, teaching both magical theory and its application. According to its official documents, the Brotherhood was founded in 1870 but did not make a public appearance until 1884, a few years before the creation of the Esoteric Section of the Theosophical Society. Its activity beforehand, if any, is unknown. However, while the H.B. of L. might only appear in the nineteenth century, the Brotherhood's teachings dated its ultimate genesis to around 600 BCE. This conveniently made the H.B. of L. the oldest existing fraternity, more than rivaling the age of Freemasonry.

Much as with the appearance of the Rosicrucian Manifestoes, the Brotherhood appeared publicly through a publication; a translation of the *Divine Pymander of Hermes Mercurius Trismegistus*, part of the *Corpus Hermeticum*, a collection of second-century CE religio-philosophical texts. As with the Rosicrucians, the Brotherhood's publication invited interested parties to write to the Brotherhood for contact. Unlike the Rosicrucians, we know that contact was actually made. While men dominated the European branch of the order, women dominated the American.[200]

Little is known about the members of the Brotherhood and there are no surviving records of membership. Once an aspirant was accepted, they were sent a series of documents that contained the teachings of the Brotherhood which would prepare them for initiation. The aspirant would also have a mentor, who was typically a member already known to them. Given the relatively small number of practicing occultists in England at the time, it was likely that any such mentor, and even the aspirant, may have

---

200 See Godwin 3. Godwin's book is the single major source for information on the H.B. of L. As such, I have made constant reference to it in this chapter.

already belonged to another esoterically leaning organization. This is the case, for instance, with the Reverend William Alexander Ayton,[201] who would also become an adept of the Order of the Golden Dawn.

The people behind the H.B. of L.'s development and organization were Max Theon, its Grand Master of the Exterior Circle, Rev. Ayton, the Provincial Grand Master of the South, and Peter Davidson, the Provincial Grand Master of the North. Davidson, also a noted Theosophist, moved to the United States in 1886,[202] extending the Brotherhood's reach to the New World, as well as eventually into France.

The second origination date of the H.B. of L., 1870, conveniently puts the Brotherhood ahead of the Theosophical Society, which was founded in 1875. When the Brotherhood appeared to the public in 1884, it directly rivaled the TS. The Brotherhood taught magical techniques and psychic abilities similar to those taught by the Theosophical Society. The H.B. of L. also used sex in its practices and effectively acted as a mockery of the TS. The Theosophical Society had taught about a Brotherhood of Luxor, which was presumably unrelated to the H.B. of L.

However, unlike the Theosophical Society, the Hermetic Brotherhood of Luxor was not Eastern-oriented. By connecting itself to Luxor, it saw itself as part of the Western *philosophia perennis*.[203] The Brotherhood was not, however, just an ideological rival to the TS but a practical one. For instance, in 1886, most of the American Control Board of the TS joined the H.B. of L. The rivalry was great enough that Blavatsky founded an Eastern or Esoteric School in the TS, which claimed to teach practical magic, though, in practice, there was more thinking

---

201 See Godwin 4.

202 Ibid. 4–5.

203 Despite sixth- to fifth-century BCE Luxor, which, as Thebes was under Assyrian control, was in no way Western.

than doing.[204] The TS wasn't the only place from which the Brotherhood drew inspiration (or plagiarized its papers). It is likely its teachings on sexual magic and magic mirrors came from the African-American occultist Paschal Beverly Randolph, founder of the Brotherhood of Eulis in 1870.[205]

Unlike Spiritualism, Theosophy, and Masonry, the Hermetic Brotherhood of Luxor had no explicit, or even implicit, "calling" toward social or political reform. Instead, as a magical order, it focused on just that—the practice of magic. The teachings were derived, often without credit, from others such as Randolph or Blavatsky, but were also created by the Brotherhood's two Provincial Grand Masters. The teachings provided to the aspirant would eventually allow them to develop enough psychic ability to make direct contact with the Brotherhood's Interior Circle, which would provide the practitioner with direct transmissions of occult knowledge, similar to the TS's Hidden Masters.[206]

The metaphysics and technical language of the H.B. of L. were drawn from the Greek language of the *Corpus Hermeticum*. The Brotherhood taught that humans were composed of spirit, soul, and body. The spirit was divine and immortal. The soul, much as in Aristophanes's speech in Plato's *Symposium*, began as bisexual, with the two halves being separated before incarnation. The soul incarnated in an attempt to reunite itself. Once incarnate, it could find its mate and realize its true nature or choose a life of materiality and further forget itself.[207] A soul that found its other half could integrate itself through the sexuo-magical practices of the Brotherhood, and presumably no longer needed to incarnate.

The Brotherhood had three grades, two of which were associated with adepthood, which constituted the Exterior

---

204 See Godwin 6–7.

205 Ibid. 40. Teachings from the Brotherhood of Eulis, which will not be discussed here, can be found in Randolph's Magia Sexualis: Sexual Practices for Magical Power.

206 Ibid. 50.

207 Ibid. 51.

and Interior Circles, where practical magic was taught. The first grade was called the Grade of Eros, the second the Ansairetic Arcanum, and the third the Mystery of Isis. Each grade was divided into three degrees for a total of nine; reminiscent of the earlier Rosicrucian orders. Of these grades, only texts from the Exterior Circle survive. It was in this grade the adept learned to control, and eventually surpass, the "elemental spheres" and the "astro-magnetic currents," which functioned like the TS's etheric and astral planes. The fully proficient adept of the Exterior Circle was a perfected human. The adept who had fully mastered and transcended this world would undergo dissolution (i.e., physical death), and enter the Interior Circle, the second grade of adeptship. Members of the Interior Circle were thought of as divine and angelic beings, beyond human comprehension.[208]

The central teachings of the H.B. of L. revolved around sex. This marked the Brotherhood as exceedingly different from its main competition. The TS's taught that sex was an unfortunate necessity of physical incarnation, but not something integral to either the soul or its spiritual progress. The H.B. of L's teachings about the soul placed sex in the center of its practices. The Brotherhood's writings even went so far as to condemn the "fearful practices in the East, of asceticism, celibacy, self-mutilations, etc., [which] simply starve and chain the animal into subjection, instead of developing it into a useful, obedient and most highly important factor of the perfect man's seven-fold nature."[209] This was not simply a criticism of the perceived practices of Buddhism and Hinduism, but a not-so-subtle attack on the TS.[210]

For the Brotherhood, sex was vital to human spiritual evolution. It was the sexual secretions and seminal fluids produced during intercourse that, when properly understood and utilized, could be used to construct the spiritual body. Love, the attraction to another, was the principle through which selfishness is

---

208 See Godwin 68–69.

209 Quoted in Godwin 70.

210 "Perhaps."

overcome. Most importantly, through sex, the soul was able to contact the higher divine powers. Even if one's sexual partner was not the other half of one's sundered soul, if operating on the same plane, sexual intercourse could still enable the soul to progress spiritually. To this end, the H.B. of L. often encouraged married couples to join the Brotherhood at the same time.[211]

Ultimately, the H.B. of L. fell. The Theosophical Society successfully presented the Brotherhood as practitioners of dark sex magic, replete with both sexual depravity and illicit drug use. These were damning traits and the Brotherhood was often seen by outsiders as little more than a fraudulent scheme bent on money making. That many of their teachings were "derived," typically without credit, from other esoteric organizations didn't help. The H.B. of L. ceased functioning before the turn of the century.

AN INTERLUDE WITH THE ORDO TEMPLI ORIENTIS (OTO)

The Ordo Templi Orientis, literally "Order of Temple of the East," is an esoteric order that still exists today. Styled after Masonry, and even attempting to include Masonic degrees after 1917, the OTO was founded in 1896 by Karl Kellner, a high-ranking Freemason, and inherited by Theodor Reuss, whom we've already seen connected to the Masonic Rite of Memphis and Misraim. Much of what is talked about today concerning the OTO is beyond the scope of this work, as it deals with the magician Aleister Crowley and his esoteric religion known as Thelema, which did not begin to fully affect the OTO until after 1917. The early history of the OTO is somewhat less sensational but nevertheless important, as it represents an outlet for Victorian occultists and has connections to Freemasonry, the Rite of Memphis and Misraim, the Brotherhood of Eulis, as well as (indirectly) to Martinism.

---

211 See Godwin 70–72.

The Ordo Templi Orientis represented one manifestation of occult Templarism, similar in some respects to Masonic Templarism. The work of Martinez de Pasqually, discussed in the next section, had connections to Fabré-Palaprat's Order of the Temple, with Pasqually's Élus Coëns and Fabré-Palaprat's Templars influencing one another. These connections, along with the writing of French occultist, Eliphas Lévi, and the legend that the Templars were an initiatory order founded by members of a Gnostic sect, inspired the formation of the OTO.[212]

Karl Kellner was a wealthy ironmaster who traveled the world in search of esoteric wisdom. Kellner believed the true secret of the Templars was a form of sexual magic. He claimed to have retrieved these secrets through sexual-yogic teachings he claimed to have received from three "oriental adepts." The system, whether he learned it from "oriental adepts," created it himself, or learned it through some other manner, holds similarities to forms of Tantra and Sufism.[213] Upon Kellner's death, Theodor Reuss inherited the Order. By 1912, the purportedly Masonic *Oriflamme*, which would publish many flattering things about the OTO, published the following on the Order's behalf, providing a hint as to the nature of the OTO's true secret: "Our Order possesses the KEY which opens up all Masonic and Hermetic secrets, namely, the teaching of sexual magic, and this teaching explains, without exception, all the secrets of Freemasonry and all systems of religion."[214]

The Order's secrets were taught through a Masonic-like degree system, consisting of twelve degrees, two of which were administrative, as well as a probationary 0°. The first three of these, after the 0°, were modeled after Blue Lodge Masonry. Members during Kellner's time would often have belonged to other esoteric organizations and would be been familiar with Cabbalah, Hermeticism, and other, similar occult traditions.

---

212 See King 17.

213 Ibid. 19.

214 Ibid. 21.

MARTINISM

While a number of modern esoteric traditions owe their birth to the TS's Eastern reorientation, this can hardly be said for all of them. Martinism, unlike the H.B. of L., the OTO, and the Golden Dawn, predates both Theosophy and Queen Victoria, having been founded in the late eighteenth century. This mystical and theurgic tradition was founded by Martinez de Pasqually. Martinism was, and is, a tradition of esoteric Christianity, though not all modern orders require members to be Christian.

The history of Martinism, or, in this case, Martinezism, is difficult. Today there are many different Martinist orders, some of which, of course, claim to be the *real* order. What is so difficult is that this seems to be true of Martinism in general, not just its modern-day iterations. From very early on, a number of different Martinist orders appeared with claims, of varying legitimacy, of lineage from Pasqually. This, in part, has to do with the work done by Louis Claude de Saint-Martin, Pasqually's student and secretary, as well as that of the Victorian Martinist Gérard Encausse.

Martinez de Pasqually was born in Grenoble, France, sometime between 1709 and 1727. Pasqually's father was a Mason and had a patent to create Masonic lodges, this, and the position of Deputy Grand Master, was passed onto his son, suggesting that Pasqually was a Master Mason by the time he was twenty-eight.[215] Martinism may have begun as an organization for Christian Masons to gather and approach their craft from a more religious position. To this end, Pasqually created the "Ordre des Chevaliers Maçons Élus Coëns de l'Univers," the Order of Knight Masons, Elect Priests of the Universe, or more simply the Élus Coëns, around 1766.[216]

Others have suggested that the Élus Coëns was foremost an order of spiritual chivalry, Pasqually having come from a

---

215 See Davis 2–3. The evidence for this, however, is lacking (Ravignat 16).
216 See Davis 2–3.

lineage of warriors and the European aristocratic military class. Every Knight Mason was "a warrior outwardly fighting against the negative forces of the prevaricated spirits."[217] Pasqually also saw regular Masonry as being fundamentally mistaken in its teachings. Regular, or as he put it "apocryphal," Masons who became Knight Masons had to renounce their former practice and were reobligated into the Élus Coëns.[218] It wasn't just reobligated apocryphal Masons who joined the order. Being ahead of his time, Pasqually also admitted women into the Élus Coëns, though these were mostly the wives of his high-ranking disciples, or women of noble birth.[219]

The initiation rituals were a combination of Masonic-style ritual and ceremonial magic. There were invocations of angels, Catholic-style rites and prayers, magical recitations of the Psalms, magic circles, Cabbalah, and so on. The purpose of all this was a spiritual reintegration or salvation through theurgy. Pasqually wrote about this in the "Treatise on the Reintegration of Beings." This described a Gnostic-styled cosmology and cosmogony.[220] Humanity, in the form of Adam, was emanated rather than created by the Creator, after the image of the Creator. Perverse or corrupted spirits influenced and corrupted Adam, causing him to act against the divine will, and thus reject the divine aspect of himself. This brought Adam, and humanity, into incarnation in the flesh.[221] The work of Martinism was the reintegration of humanity with its spiritual or divine nature.[222] Pasqually died in 1774, and the Élus Coëns didn't survive long after his death. However, two of his

---

217 See Ravignat 16.

218 Ibid. 17–18.

219 Ibid. 22–23.

220 Descriptions of what the universe it and how it was created. For comparison, see the Gnostic Apocryphon of John.

221 See Pasqually 1–7.

222 As is that of Kabbalah, and Sufism, and the TS, and the Golden Dawn… do I need to go on?

disciples would carry on the work of reintegration: Jean-Baptiste Willermoz and Louis Claude de Saint-Martin.

Willermoz was a Mason of high standing and would combine Masonic teachings, especially those of the Rite of Strict Observance, which claimed lineage from the Knights Templar, with those of Pasqually. The founder of this Rite believed he had been initiated by Charles Stuart, aka Bonnie Prince Charlie, the same person who had also granted Pasqually's father his Masonic patent. Willermoz believed he saw the beginning of the dissolution of the Élus Coëns with the death of its founder and tried to preserve as much of its teachings within his own Chevaliers bienfaisant de la Cité sainte (CBCS.).[223]

Louis Claude de Saint-Martin, eventually to be known as the Unknown Philosopher, was born of French nobility on January 18, 1743.[224] He joined the Élus Coëns at the age of twenty-five and was Pasqually's personal secretary until 1771. Whereas Willermoz embraced the ceremonial magical elements of the Élus Coëns, Saint-Martin preferred more internal approaches, which he called the "Way of the Heart." This view held that reintegration came through realizing Christ as the Word, which was with humanity from the time of creation, but had been lost.[225] Saint-Martin would eventually leave Masonry, the Élus Coëns, and the CBCS to pursue his contemplative Way of the Heart.[226] However, this didn't happen until after he opened a number of Martinist Lodges.

Saint-Martin would also make changes to Martinism's degree structure. In France and the US, the first three degrees would, for some time, even be conferred in Masonic Lodges. By the late nineteenth century, Martinism's degree structure settled into three primary degrees (possibly influenced by Masonry) and

---

223 Davis 4–6.

224 See Waite 17.

225 See Davis 7. Cf. Waite 32–34 and 46.

226 See Davis 8.

four subsidiary degrees.[227] These are the degrees of Associate, Initiate, and S∴ I∴, along with an administrative S∴ I∴ I∴ or IV degree. The last three degrees are simply numbered V–VII.[228] The degrees of Associate and Initiate focused on learning. The S∴ I∴, or *Supérieur Inconnu*, degree allowed a Martinist to initiate others into the first and second degrees. Those S∴ I∴ I∴'s who had shown dedication to the Order were given the V degree, that of Free Initiator, which allowed them to initiate others into the S∴ I∴ degree.

Many combined Willermoz's and Saint-Martin's versions of Martinism into different elements or temples within the same order. This often included a Rosicrucian element, such as seen in the Order Kabbalistique de Rose + Croix. This order was found as its own subsection of any number of Martinist Orders and was the seventh degree of the Élus Coëns.[229] All of this, however, appears to have come to a stop during the French Revolution.

The modern structure of Martinism was developed not by Saint-Martin or Willermoz, but by a relative latecomer, Gérard Encausse, better known as Papus.[230] In 1891, Papus claimed to have refounded the Martinist Order after having been passed the lineage from two Martinists claiming direct lineage to Saint-Martin. The lineage was passed through what was termed *"L'Initiation,"* which was not the rituals of induction of earlier Martinism but more like a laying on of hands. In Papus's case, it was also "an oral transmission of a particular teaching and a certain comprehension of the laws of the Universe and of Spiritual life, which, in no case could be regarded as an

---

227 See Blitz 4.

228 See Blitz 5.

229 The Élus Coëns had eleven degrees.

230 Modern Martinism is also indebted to Robert Amberlain. However, Amberlain, being a twentieth-century Martinist, is outside the scope of this work.

Initiation in a ritualistic form."[231] Papus would combine his order, originally *"L'Ordre des Supérieurs Inconnus,"*[232] and eventually *"L'Ordre Martiniste,"* with other popular esoteric movements of the time—especially Jules Doinel's revived Gnostic Church, which became Martinism's official church, just as the Johannite Church was the official church of Fabré-Palaprat's Templar order. Papus was likely also made a bishop of the Gnostic Church,[233] which would have involved its own rite of laying on of hands.

In this reconstruction of Martinism, Papus gathered a grand council of twelve to govern *L'Ordre des Supérieurs Inconnus.* Amongst those was the French occultist and novelist Joséphin Péladan.[234] Péladan's occult activities included both Martinism and Rosicrucianism. Péladan, along with the poet Stanislas de Guaita, constructed an occult Rosicrucian order. This was based both upon the extant Rosicrucian manifestos and the writings of Eliphas Lévi, who would also be influential on important members of the Golden Dawn. The building, or rebuilding from Péladan's perspective, of the Rosicrucian Order was accomplished in part through the work of Papus himself. Péladan also held a number of Rosicrucian Salons known as the *Salons de la Rose + Croix.* These were arts and music salons held in Paris in the 1890s, featuring Rosicrucian-themed artwork, poetry and literary readings, plays, musical performances, and more.

Martinism began with connections to, and similarities with, Masonry, and while some of that changed, such as the allowing of women into the order, the changes made by Papus brought Martinism perilously close to Masonry in form, making it seem to some as a kind of irregular Masonry, which may have led to its decline. This also led to almost the whole of the North American branch of the Order breaking away from Papus's

---

231 Milko Bogaard as quoted in Davis 9.

232 The Order of Unknown Superiors.

233 See Davis 8–10 and Waite 71–72.

234 Péladan would eventually leave the council.

Supreme Council in Paris,[235] and schisms became something of the norm for later Martinism. After Papus's death in the early twentieth century, we find dozens of Martinist orders.[236] Many required members to be Christian, and while others did not, all made heavy use of Christian symbolism.

The actual work of Martinism, especially under Pasqalley and Willemoz, was ritual-oriented in nature, with Saint-Martin adding a contemplative element. The rituals of Martinism were theurgic in nature, engaging in divine work, and had the appearance of a cross between medieval ceremonial magic and Masonic ritual. The initiations were similar in style, if not in content, to Masonic initiations. Regalia included robes, cloaks, sashes, and masks. The teachings of Martinism included elements, philosophical and practical, of Hermeticism, Gnosticism, Neoplatonism, Cabbalah, and more, and are so connected more to forms of esotericism like that of the Golden Dawn than to mainstream Masonry.

THE ORDER OF THE GOLDEN DAWN AND THE ROSÆ RUBEÆ ET AUREÆ CRUCIS

The Order of the Golden Dawn (GD) is possibly the most well-known magical order in the English-speaking world. This is due to a number of reasons, including its overall influence on modern Western occultism, the dramas which took place within the Order and its various schismatic offshoots, and the number of figures who were, and continue to be, important outside of occultism. This includes one of Ireland's most famous poets William Butler Yeats, women's rights activist Maude Gonne, the actress Florence Farr, and Annie Horniman, one of the founders of repertory theatre.

---

235 See Waite 77.
236 See Bogaard.

Although publicly appearing in 1888, the story of the Golden Dawn goes back somewhat further. We will start with Dr. William Wynn Westcott, one of the three founders of the order, along with Dr. William Robert Woodman and Samuel Liddell Mathers. Westcott was a Master Mason, a Martinist, a Theosophist, and by 1882, the General Secretary of the Soc. Ros., the degree structure of which would influence that of the GD.

In 1887, Westcott claimed to have discovered a set of manuscripts, written in a well-known occult cipher, amongst the possessions of the recently deceased Mason, Reverend A.F.A. Woodford. The manuscripts, which contained the outlines of several initiation rituals and some basic occult information, may have been written by Kenneth R.H. Mackenzie, one of the founders of the Soc. Ros.[237] Westcott believed Mackenzie received an authentic Rosicrucian initiation in Austria[238] and had the right to found new Rosicrucian orders.

The connection between Westcott and Mackenzie is strong. Not only did Westcott take over some of Mackenzie's occult offices upon the latter's death, but Westcott was a member of Mackenzie's Order of Eight, with which the manuscripts may have been associated.[239] However, Mackenzie followed strict Masonic protocol with his esoteric orders and did not allow women to join. Westcott, having been influenced by both Martinism and the renowned English occultist Anna Kingsford and her Hermetic Society, of which Westcott was an honorary member, believed the inclusion of women in esoteric societies was absolutely necessary.[240]

Having outlines of initiation rituals through the cipher manuscripts, Westcott hired the young Freemason Samuel Mathers, later styling himself "MacGregor," to decipher the manuscripts

---

237 See Gilbert's Scrapbook 31.

238 See Gilbert's Twilight 15.

239 See Gilbert's Scrapbook 5–6.

240 Ibid. 5.

and work up the outlines into full rituals. It is unclear as to why Westcott needed Mathers to do this; Westcott both had access to the cipher's key and was an accomplished ritualist. It is possible, Mathers being in something of a perpetual state of financial distress, that Westcott felt it was his Masonic duty to help his Brother, and this was one way to do so. Regardless of the reason, Mathers produced a set of five initiation rituals from the manuscripts. Based along Masonic lines, especially the first two degrees, the rituals would form the initiatory backbone of the Order of the Golden Dawn.

Where Masonic initiations brought the candidate through a symbolic passage through King Solomon's Temple, the Golden Dawn's rituals symbolically raised the candidate through the different levels of the Qabalistic Tree of Life. However, the initiations were not understood as being simply symbolic and allegorical. These rituals were, as with Martinism's, magical or theurgic in nature, and were believed to cause real changes to the candidate on unseen levels.[241]

Besides the ritual outlines, the ciphers contained a list of occult subjects to study, which Westcott worked up into "knowledge lectures" for each of the GD's grades.[242] The lectures consisted of a course of study of theoretical knowledge, as well as the Lesser Ritual of the Pentagram. Initiates studied hermetic Cabbalah, astrology, alchemy, multiple forms of divination, the formation of magical sigils, the planets, the zodiac, the various spirits and angels associated with them, and more.[243] Like Masonry, each grade had a password and handshake, as well as a sash denoting the magician's grade.

---

241 The most common source for Golden Dawn information is Israel Regardie's The Golden Dawn, which exists in multiple editions, with a new one released in 2016.

242 See Zalewski 20.

243 See Gilbert's Scrapbook 62–63.

The ciphers also included the address for a woman called S. D. A., later understood to stand for *Sapiens Dominabitur Astris*, Fraulein Anna Sprengel. Sprengel, assuming she actually existed,[244] was a member of the original German Rosicrucian order. It was she who, according to Westcott, gave Westcott, Mathers, and Woodman the grade of 7=4, Exempt Adept, and the authority to form a new branch of the order in England.[245]

A year after opening, the primary temple of the order, Isis-Urania Temple, had gained about thirty-two members. Another fourteen were initiated in 1889. A number of members had, by 1888, gone through all of the Outer Order material and initiations, and had been admitted into the Inner Order. However, this didn't actually exist in any practical way; the rituals and knowledge lectures stopped with the 4=7 grade of Philosophus. Westcott and Mathers claimed the Inner Order grades of Adeptus Minor through Adeptus Exempt.[246] The latter grade was the highest grade of the Second Order or the *Rosæ Rubeæ et Aureæ Crucis* (R.R. et A.C.), "the Rose of Ruby and the Cross of Gold." The creation of the Second or Inner Order introduced a spiritual element to the GD. The Adept was to gain access to their "higher" or "divine" self, that part of the human soul which remembers, but remains in contact with, its Divinity.

The order and its three temples continued to grow, as did the Inner Order, still without initiation rituals or knowledge lectures. This changed in 1891, when Mathers and his new wife, Moina, moved to Paris. Rituals for the liminal degree of Portal and Adeptus Minor were written. The latter was reportedly received

---

244 It is believed by many that the correspondences between Westcott and Sprengel were forged by Westcott to lend credibility and lineage to his Order, as well as the authority to run it for him and Mathers. Woodman, the third founder of the Order, appeared to have done very little with it and died before the formation of the Inner Order.

245 See Gilbert's *Twilight* 28 and Farrell 28–29.

246 See Zaleweksi 32.

through contact with Mather's version of Theosophy's Hidden Masters, a Secret Chief called "Frater Lux et Tenebris," whom Mathers claimed to have met in the flesh. As a Rosicrucian degree, the Adeptus Minor ritual was based around the *Fama Fraternitatis* and contained elements of Christian mysticism. Those who had been admitted to the Adeptus Minor grade could now be officially initiated. Mathers and Westcott also worked up a great amount of degree material, both theoretical and practical. Pieces of Adeptus Minor subgrades, as well as the higher grades of Adeptus Major and Adeptus Exempt, were also written. These were not more fully developed until after numerous schisms within the order.

The esoteric knowledge learned in the higher grades greatly expanded upon the information from the Outer Order. More Qabalah was studied, often making recourse to Jewish Kabbalistic texts such as the *Zohar* and *Sefer Yetzirah*. The surviving writings of the Elizabethan magus Dr. John Dee were organized into a system of magic called "Enochian" and synthesized with the rest of the order's teachings. The magical elements of the initiation rituals were expanded upon and formalized, especially in the case of the Neophyte ritual. A new system of tarot, along with a new tarot deck designed especially for the order, was created.[247] Eschewing skrying through mirrors, which the H.B. of L. had used, a method of astral projection and "skrying through the spirit vision" was created. Through this practice, the adept could view the astral plane and associated elemental, planetary, zodiacal, or sefirotic[248] realms. An adept could magically consecrate tools, invoke and command the powers of the elements and planets, consecrate talismans, converse with angels, and, at higher grades, control demons.

---

247 If you've looked at a tarot deck produced after A. E. Waite's Rider-Waite deck, which was modeled on the Golden Dawn's deck, it was likely influenced by the GD, even if the deck's creator didn't know it.

248 The ten sefirot, spelled within the order as "sephiroth," make up, along with twenty-two connecting paths, the Tree of Life.

All this information was parceled out in a systematized format of grades and subgrades. Each subgrade had a set of tests, both theoretical and practical. During the era of the original order, only a few of the Adeptus Minor subgrades had been developed, those of Zelator and Theoricus Adeptus Minor, and the latter not completely. After the schisms of the early twentieth century, changes were made to the grade system, and new grade material was created, especially in the New Zealand branch.

Beginning in 1900, after years of growth, the Order of the Golden Dawn began to see the beginning of its end. Some of this came about due to differences between Mathers and Westcott. Mathers is often described in terms of megalomania and had a domineering and totalitarian personality. In his largely one-sided feud with Westcott, Mathers related to Florence Farr, an adept and temple Chief, that Westcott had forged the letters from S. D. A. and it was he, Mathers, who was really in contact with the Chiefs of the Order. Trust in Westcott deteriorated after this, and Westcott would eventually resign from the Order, supposedly because Mathers left Order documents with Westcott's name on them in a taxi. As Westcott was a Crown Coroner, his association with a magical order wouldn't do.[249]

But this wasn't the only problem. The various adepts and Temple Chiefs became increasingly resentful of Mathers's authoritarianism. When he initiated the young Aleister Crowley into the grade of Adeptus Minor against the wishes of the Chiefs at the Isis-Urania Temple, rebellion occurred. Crowley was considered an immoral dilatant by the Isis-Urania Chiefs, and he and Mathers were expelled from the Order; Mathers also in part for his role in Westcott's forgeries. In response, Mathers counter-expelled the Chiefs, claiming that they hadn't the authority to expel him, which did nothing to stop them from doing so. There was also a legal scandal involving some

---

249 The English royals have a long history in Freemasonry, so this would not have been an issue.

American charlatans which dragged the Order's name into the light and through the mud.[250]

Due to all these factors, the Order of the Golden Dawn effectively ceased to exist. In its place rose new, and largely identical, orders. These held allegiances to various personalities from the GD, though individual members were often in communication with members from other offshoots. Mathers called his order the Alpha et Omega (AO). A. E. Waite, who was a member of the Isis-Urania temple, formed a revised, and more Christian, version of the Order called the Holy Order of the Golden Dawn. Other Isis-Urania adepts reformed under the name *Morgen Röth*, the Red Dawn. Others formed the Stella Matutina (SM), including Dr. Robert Felkin. When Felkin moved to New Zealand, following promptings from his own contacts with the Secret Chiefs, he founded the Smaragdum Thalasses Temple, the Emerald of the Sea.

From these, almost countless other GD-styled orders formed, though unlike the AO or SM, without chartered lineage to the original Order. Eventually, all of the original schism groups would shut their doors, the AO in the 1950s, the SM in the 1960s in England, and the 1970s in New Zealand.[251] Today, there are a number of groups using the name of the Golden Dawn or its offshoots. While some claim direct chartered lineage to the original order, and especially to Mathers, no evidence of this has ever been forthcoming.

In the more than one hundred years of existence of the Golden Dawn and its schisms, there have been many members. A list of those gleaned from surviving records of members shows a few hundred people.[252] These came from all walks of life: doctors,

---

250 See Zaleweksi 38.

251 Ibid. 39–42.

252 Cf. Küntz 171–221. A number of famous people who never belonged to the Order, such as Bram Stoker and Sir Arthur Conan Doyle, have later been "added" to the rosters.

scholars, clergy, actresses, poets, artists, and just about anyone else who could read and write and had an interest in not only studying the occult but practicing it.

The main force driving the Golden Dawn, at least until 1900, was the man who fleshed out the initiation rituals from the cipher manuscripts, Samuel Lidell "MacGregor" Mathers.[253] We know relatively little about Mathers's early life. He likely came from a working-class English family and may have spent some time in the military, with which he was obsessed. From a financial perspective, Mathers never amounted to much. He had a hard time keeping jobs and often relied on the goodness, and wealth, of members of the Order for his and his wife's upkeep, even though Moina was a very talented artist. In the occult world, Mathers was a genius, even if an unstable one. He was versed in both Kabbalah and Qabalah, astrology, tarot, geomancy, the works of John Dee and Henry Cornelius Agrippa, and more. After 1900, the Mathers spent most of their time in Paris and held performances of the Rites of Isis and Osiris, possibly inspired by Péladan's Salons de la Rose + Croix from a decade earlier.

One of the most prominent members of the GD outside of its founders was Florence Farr.[254] Farr was an English actress of great repute and should be known to any student of British theater, regardless of their interest in the occult. Farr married young and soon discovered she hated the life of a Victorian married woman.[255] Her husband ended their marriage after a scandal in 1888 and moved to the US. Farr never tied herself to anyone again. She had a notable acting career and associated with

---

253 For a full biography of Mathers, see Nick Farrell's King Under the Water.

254 For biographies on Florence Farr, Moina Mathers, Maude Gonne, and Annie Horniman—not just four of the most prominent female members of the Order, but four of the most prominent members of the Order, full stop—see Mary K. Greer's Women of the Golden Dawn.

255 See Mary K. Greer 25–26.

some of the UK's best and brightest, such as George Bernard Shaw and the Irish poet W. B. Yeats. These figures did not create Farr's career, but they did enhance it.[256] Farr wasn't limited to acting, she was also a director, producer, and composer. Outside of the theater, she was a women's rights activist, suffragette, and journalist.

Farr entered the Golden Dawn in 1890 through her association with "Willie" Yeats. Just as on the stage and in her nontheatrical life, Farr excelled at what she did. She became an adept, wrote a number of Inner Order papers, and replaced Westcott as a Chief of the Order when he resigned. She was also Mathers's personal representative in England until she co-led the schism against him. She left the Order in 1892 and joined the Theosophical Society. She continued to act, write, and produce and was involved with Yeats's famous Abby Theatre. All through this, she worked for women's rights, going so far as to sell all her possessions, move to Ceylon, and take up teaching in a school for girls, which was her first vocation. Farr died in 1917 from breast cancer.

William Butler Yeats is perhaps the most well-known of the Golden Dawn adepts. Like Farr, this is not due to his association with the Order but his work outside it, as a poet and playwright. Still, much like Farr's, Yeats's writing was heavily influenced by his occult work, as well as his interest in Irish mythology. Although Yeats had a close association with Mathers, he, like many of the London adepts, severed ties with him during the schism. Yeats then helped lead the Isis-Urania Temple, though Farr was perhaps the real power behind it. Yeats's magical notebooks and implements are held by the National Library of Ireland.

There are, of course, others to write about. Westcott was a brilliant occultist in his own right. Although he was overshadowed by Mathers's personality, a great deal of the Inner Order material has since been attributed to him rather than Mathers.

---

256 Farr spent time as Shaw's mistress. Let's just say it didn't stick.

Suffering from what we might call the "occultist's complaint" (i.e., asthma), Westcott retired in 1910 and moved to South Africa. Moina Mathers was a highly skilled artist and likely developed the complex system of color used in the Inner Order. Upon Mathers's death, she became the head of AO. The list of famous and semi-famous members of the Order is extensive, and each such person was important to the world outside of their occult work, and often in spite of it. More importantly, what we see for each of these people is that their occultism bled over and influenced their everyday lives. For these magicians, magic was not something they did, it was part of who they were.

SOCIAL INVOLVEMENT?

As we've seen, many Spiritualists were also active feminists, suffragettes, and, in the US, abolitionists. Many members of the Theosophical Society followed suit, and the TS itself had feminism structured into its roots. While Masonry did not engage in women's rights movements, it, like many other fraternal orders, had a strong hand in social welfare, charity, and relief. This all seems to stop with the magical orders.

To a certain extent, such orders, all of which were in some way influenced by Masonry, took on Masonry's motto of "making good men better," though perhaps without the gender limitations. But while this might have been a side-effect of magic and initiation, it was not the goal of the work of the adept and their higher genius or soul.

However, this isn't the end of it. Although individual members of magical orders might have engaged in different forms of social activism, the orders themselves typically did not. Instead, the spiritual progress of the magician or theurgist would bring about a bettering of the conditions of those around them. Such adepts understood themselves as conduits for the divine light into the world.

Besides being the equivalent of a spiritual flashlight, there are examples of adepts making more specific attempts to improve the world through magical means. One of the most notable examples of this was Florence Farr's "Sphere Group," a secret group within the R.R. et A.C. The group did two things. First, it attempted to channel new teachings from the Order's Secret Chiefs. Second, to bring about world peace, members used meditation and visualization to project the Tree of Life in three dimensions over and around the Earth.[257] This expanded to a magical visualization of a grail-like cup through which they projected divine light onto the whole world while attempting to transmute forces of evil into agents of good.[258] This is the social involvement magical orders did, with "society" being the entire world.

CHARACTER SKETCH: THE SORCERER

The Chevalier Sèitheach MacGregor, PhD, GSRA, OT, etc., etc., etc. is my steamsona. A sorcerer and necromancer, Sèitheach was born in Strathmore, Scotland, in the year of our Lord 1411. Having made a deal with a planetary spirit, he extended his life to some nine hundred years and has generally been enjoying himself ever since. Sèitheach has learned from bog witches and sorceresses as well as the likes of Dr. John Dee, Paracelsus, and Marsilio Ficino. He became the Grand Prior of the Order of the Ruby Ankh around 1785 because he missed a meeting and they voted him in. A serious student of the occult arts, he rarely takes himself seriously. Sèitheach can occasionally be found wandering around steampunk conventions lecturing on various occult subjects, while offering scathing reviews of pretty much everything, including himself. Failing that, he'll be in the Tea Room.

---

257 See King 74.
258 Ibid. 257.

Sèitheach wears a variation of traditional Scottish dress. His argyle jacket holds the medals of the orders of knighthood to which he has been admitted, the symbol of the Order of the Ruby Ankh, and has a number of snarky badges. He wears the MacGregor tartan, a nod to S. L. Mathers, and a variety of waistcoats. His top hat displays the Eye of Ra (spelled "Re" in academic context) and a number of tarot cards. His walking stick glows with the light of the Ruby Ankh—or at least an LED hidden in the crystal top. His cravat and spats are embroidered with magical symbols from the Key of Solomon.

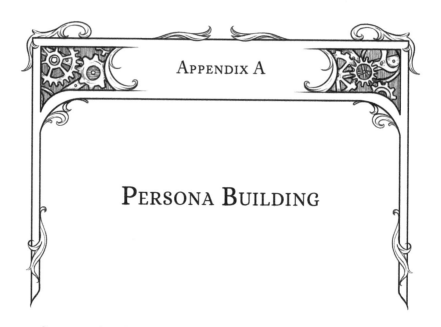

Persona Building

Steampunk, taken to its fullest, is an immersive activity. There are still novels, movies, and comics based in, on, or around steampunk themes. Steampunks, however, typically go beyond these in their expressions of Victoriana. More recently, there are steampunk-themed cookbooks and craft books, and sewing pattern and fabric companies have started marketing to us as well. Steampunk music is a thing, too, though there isn't always agreement on what makes music steampunk. This is true of steampunk in general. All of this is because, like goths and punks and metalheads, we don't simply read or watch the genre, we try to live it. This can occur in many different settings: one's daily life, special meetings with friends or an airship crew, or, increasingly, steampunk conventions.

There are currently a number of steampunk conventions in the US and a growing number abroad. Some of these are the typical conventions; a bunch of people milling about, some in costume, some not, listening to panels on various subjects. Others are immersive events,[259] with actors and plotlines, with events

---

259 The largest of these immersive events is TeslaCon, held near Madison, Wisconsin, takes place annually.

occurring throughout the con. At such conventions, almost everyone, attendees and cast, are dressed in steampunk attire[260] and, just as importantly, many of the attendees have a steamsona.

A steamsona is a second, or for some people, a third or fourth, self—the protagonist in your live-action steampunk adventure. As discussed in Chapter One, "steamsona" is a play on words based on the Latin word *persōna,* meaning "a mask or character." Originally, *persona* referred to a character played by an actor. Later, the psychiatrist Carl Gustav Jung used it to refer to the different masks we wear, consciously or not, to interact with the world. A steampunk persona, a steamsona, is somewhere in between. Importantly, a steamsona is in no way required to be a steampunk. You can go to a convention or other event as yourself and have a perfectly wonderful time. Some find the experience of being someone else enhances their enjoyment, others not so much. Neither way is superior, they are simply different ways to enjoy steampunk. The preceding chapters present you with a lot of information. In the bibliography, there are more resources to be better acquainted with whichever topics you'd like to use in bringing your steamsona to life.

WHAT KIND OF PERSONA?

As you've seen, Victorian esotericisms had ways of transcending social norms and statuses. Many Spiritualists, especially the more well-known ones, were often originally from lower social classes. Many ceremonial magicians lived firmly in the middle class, but this was hardly a rule. Nobility continues to dot the ranks of Freemasonry in England, and the clergy are found almost everywhere. Steampunks of a more scientific bent often form personae from the middle or upper class, but the crew of an airship, the way many steampunk groups gather and present themselves, often has people from all walks of life. If you

---

260 This is in no way required. Enjoying yourself is the priority, not trying to fit in.

don't like corsets and hose or tailored suits, a more blue-collar persona may be more to your liking. After all, blue jeans existed by the mid-1800s.

Then again, many occultists were also scholars of varying skill and education. Perhaps a professor or a member of the leisure class is more to your liking. In steampunk, we try to avoid the classism of actual Victorian society so the only barriers, in terms of social position, are the ones created by your own particular interests.[261] Choose something, or someone, of interest to you and have fun. What does this all look like? That's difficult to say. Instead, you will likely know it when you see it.[262] Go with that feeling and explore. At worst, you just have to start over again.

This step should help you not only begin developing your steamsona, but it will also help you determine what kind of clothing is appropriate. If you are making or buying your wardrobe, you can start looking around for patterns or items that fit your style. Not everyone can afford clothing made just for their persona or has the skills to sew something new. If you're working on a tight budget, thrift stores are your friend. An old vest can be transformed into a waistcoat, prom dresses into nineteenth-century bustle skirts. Sometimes it's helpful to work backward starting with the clothing you have and building the persona around it.[263]

Geography is another element to consider. Where are you from? Some steampunks place their personae in their home-towns. You already know the place, so it makes playing that character easier. Many pick a persona from the United Kingdom

---

261 Social status will help you figure out what sorts of clothing will be appropriate for your persona, but so will figuring out where they're from or where they live. There are plenty of resources available on Victorian clothing, as well as numerous clothing makers with a steampunk orientation.

262 See Sirkin.

263 See Cowford Steampunk Society.

or Ireland and often see the UK as the "home" of steampunk. That isn't a reason to limit yourself to English-speaking places. England, France, and Russia were bastions of culture and esotericism at this time. If you are developing a European-based persona, and this is by no means necessary, consider that many Europeans were born abroad. Nothing requires your steamsona to be from Earth, either. When considering all this, always be careful of cultural appropriation or absorbing the racism of the time. Also, while accents are one of the more enjoyable, and memorable, parts of steampunk,[264] be wary of falling into racist stereotypes.

The time period your persona is from can also be important, though it doesn't need to be. Most steampunks aren't "thread counters." We don't care if your fabric is period correct or if the distance between the eyelets on your corset are spaced the way there were in March of 1889. However, organizations and movements began and ended at specific times. If your steamsona is an adept of the Golden Dawn, having them be actively so in 1882 doesn't make a great deal of sense as the GD didn't exist then. But a secret, Golden Dawn-like order absolutely might have. Having a more specific time frame other than "Victorian" may be helpful to you in developing your persona. If so, use it; if not, don't.

Just as important as figuring out where your persona is from, geographically and socially, is determining your persona's interests, occult and otherwise. Victorian occultists tended to have their fingers in a number of different magical pies. Ceremonial magicians were often Masons. Masons were often Martinists. Almost everyone had some sort of interest in Theosophy. Rosicrucians could be modern Druids. Modern Druids might also be Masons, and Masons were sometimes Templars. Many people had an interest in Spiritualism, even if that interest

---

264 See Cowford Steampunk Society.

was negative.[265] You can also decide if your persona belongs to a particular organization, such as the Theosophical Society, or if they work alone. If they do belong to an organization (or organizations) there is no need for it to be a historical one. In fact, it is often better to create something of your own, and the information presented earlier in this book should be helpful in doing so. All of these details will help you fill out your steamsona and become immersed in it.

---

265 Initiates of the Golden Dawn were forbidden to engage in Spiritualist practices or allow themselves to be placed in passive trance or
hypnotic states.

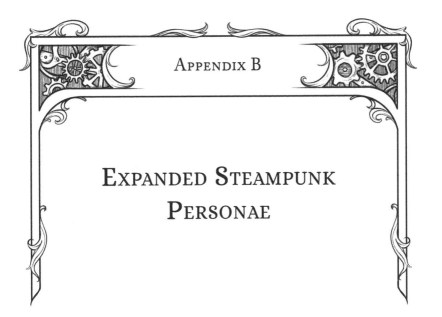

APPENDIX B

EXPANDED STEAMPUNK PERSONAE

Eight character sketches are sprinkled about in the previous pages: The Suffragette Medium, the Knight, the Rosicrucian, the Fae (both fairy and redcap), the Druid, the Cunning Woman, and the Sorcerer. Rather than being definitive in any way, these are merely examples of what one could do with such character concepts. The sketches are just that—short descriptions of steamsonas meant to inspire ideas. What follows are expanded versions of these characters. Each will discuss background concepts, aesthetics, their lives in general, and clothing suggestions. Like the sketches, these are not meant to be definitive but rather to demonstrate how one might build up a full steamsona from a concept.

When possible, I have tried to limit the clothing to what is commercially available, though varying degrees of alteration might be necessary to complete a look.

THE SUFFRAGETTE MEDIUM

Name: Francisca Beatrice Alexandra Marie Stone
Background Concept: Avant-garde, upper-class, suffragist agitator.

Ms. Stone's mother, Amelia, came from a background of wealth. Her father, Herbert, was originally a stone mason until he found himself somehow in charge of the quarries he used to work in, eventually owning them. Her mother instilled in her a sense of propriety and a need for justice. Her father taught her that the world was unfair and capricious, giving with one hand and taking away with the other. Both showed her the importance of using one's power to help those most in need, a lesson that took some time for her to learn.

The young Francisca rarely wanted for anything she actually needed, or often things she merely desired. Her life was a mix of strict regimen and opulent extravaganza. Her mother set for her a list of daily chores; her father, lessons in language, maths, and philosophy. Her social circle, all of whom came from varying degrees of Old Money, pushed her toward ever new experiences while they chased after the latest thing. Her parents rarely approved and set to showing her the consequences of her friends' lives—not in how it affected them but by showing how it affected those around them: servants, employees, shopkeepers, and the working class and poor in general. Francesca did not like what she saw. She saw how powerless others were in the face of wealth, especially women, and the advantages her parents had given her, and so she became an agitator for votes for women and equal rights in general.

Life: Ms. Stone is an ardent suffragist and works as a writer for the *Daily Sunflower*, a suffragist newspaper. Her column, "Suffrage at Home and Abroad," focuses on the successes and failures of women's movements in England and New York. Successes so that her readers know that they are making headway and to show what has worked elsewhere, failures to show what should be avoided or changed. She also helps organize local marches and rallies and other such events to agitate for the vote. It was through such a rally that she met her...roommate, Dr. Jennifer O'Toole. It was through Dr. O'Toole that she came into contact with a circle of mediums in Queens.

The Freedom of Spirit circle was formed in the spring of 1859 by a small group of psychics specializing in healing. Having been missed by herself and her parents, Dr. O'Toole sensed Francisca's hidden psychic abilities almost immediately and introduced her to the circle. These experienced mediums helped foster her abilities, her particular gift being that of diagnosis. Francisca consults at Dr. O'Toole's clinic for women and children on those cases that prove to be especially difficult to diagnose given the state of nineteenth-century medicine.

As suggested by their name, the Freedom of Spirit circle not only worked with and trained new mediums but they also were concerned with equal rights for women and other minorities. Francisca quickly connected them to other like-minded mediums, itself developing into a network, which now helps coordinate and organize rights agitators across New York.

AESTHETIC: Trendsetter with an eye for equality.

Some habits die hard, and Ms. Stone freely admits that her clothing budget is perhaps higher than it should be. She keeps track of the latest trends, in both men's and women's fashion, and promptly turns them on their ear. Merging the looks of her favorite designers, Francisca's wardrobe consists of clothing both beautiful and practical. Upon moving to New York, she quickly adopted the "American costume." However, rather than patronizing the best, which is to say, the most expensive tailors, Ms. Stone almost exclusively shopped at smaller businesses while making sure to pay as much as she would at the upper echelons of the Garment District.

While no fashion designer, Ms. Stone has employed a number of such, drawing them largely from the tailor shops she frequented, which are mostly family-run businesses. Fostering their talent by providing them access to an education they would otherwise not have, Ms. Stone has developed a line of women's clothing designed to be stylish, practical, and most importantly, affordable. The sleeves of shirts and jackets are gusseted for ease of movement, be it hoisting protest signs in the air or swinging them to ward off the police or other would-be attackers. The pants allow for quick movement away from a group of rowdy drunks or toward a mob of counter-protestors. The skirts, of course, have pockets. Her designers earn a significant commission on all pieces sold. Ms. Stone invests the rest in both the businesses that produce the clothing and the family-run textile mills from which they get their material.

Dressing the Part: Francisca's clothing style is focused on practicality. Her clothing allows her freedom of movement and limits the risk of getting caught on something while at a protest or getting in the way while consulting. For this steamsona, traditional Victorian women's clothing, especially for the upper class, is straight out. She wears no corset, no petticoat, no bustle, no dress. The closest she has to this is a pair of wide-legged pants with a front cover that makes them look like a dress. And the panel is removable.

There are at least three varieties of pants to choose from. The first is riding pants, loose-legged and meant for riding horses rather than bicycles. There are modern varieties that, as above, come with removable front panels. The second is bloomers, which feature puffed-out upper legs that end with a tight cough below the knee. Stockings or long socks are worn underneath to cover the leg. Work pants often look similar to men's trousers, though not necessarily as high-wasted. One can, of course, draw from men's clothing as well, which, from a Victorian perspective, would make a strong statement about one's sensibilities.

Blouses tend toward being loose, especially in the sleeves, which often had long, tighter cuffs done up with buttons. There are blouses with more ruffles or other fanciness, but our Ms. Stone eschews such things as they tend to make all of her jobs more difficult. Over this can be worn a vest or waistcoat, which would help keep the body of the blouse clean and reduce the odds it snags on anything, an important feature when out protesting. A Victorian woman's jacket would typically have a snug bodice and a skirt of various lengths flaring from the waist. Most women's shoes would have had a heel of some sort. Francisca boots with a low, wider heel for more stability for running or swinging picket signs.

THE KNIGHT

NAME: Henry Jonathan Thomas Brougham, III
BACKGROUND CONCEPT: Gentleman in the rough trying to build a better world.

For someone looking from the outside, a single word best describes Henry Brougham's early life: traditional. He grew up with traditional parents who had traditional working-class values and attended a traditional Anglican church. He wore the clothing, addressed and associated with people, and generally conducted himself in the way expected of his social station. The oldest of five children, he acted as a surrogate father to his siblings and followed in his father's footsteps to become a bricklayer, like five generations of his family beforehand. He expected to marry a traditional wife, have the appropriate number of children—the oldest of whom would become a bricklayer—and eventually die a traditional death given his vocation. But secretly, deep in his inner life, Henry Brougham rebelled against it all. He wanted *more*.

He learned to imitate the "Oxford" accent and could freely switch between that and his native Liverpudlian Scouse. He snuck into high Anglican churches in other neighborhoods. He even bought for himself a set of dress clothes that he probably would never get to wear in public. He read voraciously, consuming any printed material he could get his hands on—philosophy, poetry, newspapers, literature, and novels.

He particularly enjoyed the new penny dreadfuls. When not raising his siblings, doing chores, or working, Henry lived at the libraries. From there, he learned about the state of the country and the rest of the world. Henry Brougham did not like what he read.

Life: By the time he was ten, Hank, as his father's friends called him, was already a skilled bricklayer. He was generally a "good kid." He didn't get in trouble, he stayed out of the way of grownups, and generally kept his head down and trudged forward in life. But he also learned the value of money and what he could and, more importantly, couldn't do with it. He loved his parents but also respected them; they worked hard, took care of their family, and were overall kind people. It was from them, largely from his mother, Harriet, that Henry learned both how to take care of people and why it was important to do so.

When he turned eighteen, Henry's uncle took him to meet a group of Masons. Being a bricklayer, he didn't think much of it, though he was excited that he might learn a new skill or even a new trade. These, however, were not the "masons" he had expected. After a short time, Brother Arnold Alexander Brougham sponsored his nephew's entry into Freemasonry. His brothers became a second family to him, more so as he never married, or even had a long-term relationship, at least in public. When he was at his highest, they were there to celebrate with him. When he was at his lowest, such as when he lost his arm in an accident, his brothers not only supported him but got for him a mechanical arm—something he could have never afforded on his own. It was through this new family that he was able to contribute charitably on a level he couldn't have done otherwise. It was also where the Order of the Ruby Ankh found him.

Henry applied the same vigor he had for reading and charity to everything in his life. His ability to memorize was nothing short of astounding. His ritual work, Masonry's initiations being worked from memory, was perfect, and he was able to effortlessly move between offices. But he didn't just speak his lines—he empowered them and brought them to life. His sponsor in the Order saw Henry's inner nobility and his power to affect the world. He was made a Knight Companion in due course and was given access to his Priory's library. Learning the Latin necessary to read much of it was simple, though he struggled with the Greek. Through his efforts, the Priory created a charitable foundation for those who had been injured in industrial accidents and put Sir Henry Brougham in charge of it.

AESTHETIC: Bricklayer by day, Chevalier by night

Despite his age, having turned seventy last fall, Henry Brougham is still a bricklayer by trade. He expects he will be until he passes. His traditional clothing is rugged and utilitarian, with his coat, waistcoat, and pants being made from sturdy canvas. A cap covers his head, and patches, his clothing. Colors are muted as brightly dyed cloth is expensive and Henry has better places to spend his money than fashion. Every third Wednesday evening is Lodge night. While not necessarily required, Masons have tended to wear suits to Lodge, including those who are not officers and are simply in the columns. A white lambskin apron is worn over it, along with any symbols of Masonic office they might be entitled to. Brother Brougham dresses as expected and puts on his best clothing, before walking down to Grail Lodge No. 32.

Elsewhen, however, Sir Henry Jonathan Thomas Brougham III dresses any way but traditional. When on official Order business, Sir Henry dons a black hooded cloak lined in black and bearing the symbol of the Order embroidered on the right side. The Order has no dress code other than this. Henry, having been raised on stories of King Arthur, from the *Mabinogion* to Mallory, leans into the idea of knighthood as much as possible, and enjoys every moment of it. Inspired by medieval stories of Perceval, when out knighting (as he calls it), Sir Henry wears a crimson waistcoat with matching trousers and boots. He owns a small collection of ankle-length frock-styled long coats in both white and black, with wide crimson piping and golden buttons at the chest and cuff. When in what he considers his full regalia, Henry doesn't simply walk from place to place, he flows, with cloak and long coat floating around him. He has considered carrying a sword cane, but given that his mechanical hand can crush bricks, he's decided it would be redundant. Fun, though.

DRESSING THE PART: The Knight's outfit is relatively simple… except not. While long frock coats are available, unless you get them oversized, they will not be as long as what Henry is depicted in. There are a number of frock coats geared toward Masons in the York Rite's Knight Templar degrees that are commercially available, but again, nothing of this length. The length isn't important, though. The purpose of the Knight's outfit is to stand out, and any of these kinds of coats will do the trick. They typically come in plain black, so if you want some decorative piping or different buttons, those would be aftermarket additions.

Black hooded cloaks are readily available online and are also relatively simple to make if you have basic sewing skills and a machine. Henry's cloak, with the exception of the hood, is modeled on those worn by modern orders of English knights. These usually have a large, hand-embroidered symbol on their shoulder representing their order of knighthood, which is not exactly cost-friendly to the average person. If you embroider, you can work up your own symbol and apply it yourself. Otherwise, there are businesses that machine embroider custom patches.

With this sort of outfit, you have a number of options for what is worn underneath. If you do not plan on taking the coat off while in public, all you need to think about style-wise are trousers and footwear. Standard black works with pretty much everything. If you are going to take off the coat, then you'll have to decide upon a shirt and potentially a waistcoat. Again, a white shirt and black vest cover you just fine. Fancier options exist as well, including Victorian-style shirts and trousers of varying styles and colors.

THE ROSICRUCIAN

NAME: Ambrose Titus Saloman
BACKGROUND CONCEPT: Teacher and esoteric scholar bent on repaying a debt of gratitude.

Ambrose had always been a robust child. He played football and rugby growing up and even looked into going professional. Instead, he fell in love with music. Ambrose entered university in nearby Wilberforce and learned everything he could about his love. Upon graduation, he took his new degree, and his rather used cello, and left for New Paris to follow his dreams. Hailing from Dayton, Ambrose was used to being a man of color in a city of Whiteness. In New Paris, he largely blended in with the crowd. He still had more than his share of challenges, as blending in meant not standing out, and Ambrose worked odd jobs while trying to open his own school. He offered private lessons and, after a time, was successful in business, though he'd never be wealthy from what he made teaching. Ambrose soon married Ms. Althea Clark and their first child, Constanze, followed shortly thereafter.

Constanze had always been a sickly child. The doctors never could figure out what was wrong with her, but they did know she probably didn't have long to live. Her parents could afford the doctors' visits, but medicine was expensive, assuming they ever figured out how to treat her. Help never came from the doctors. Instead, it came in the form of the pharmacist whose pharmacy was beneath the Salomans's apartment. The older man simply appeared at their door one evening and offered his services, gratis. Mr. Chan examined baby Constanze for a few minutes in a way the doctors never had. He nodded to himself, disappeared downstairs, returned shortly after, and administered a golden-hued tincture. He came back five more evenings to administer the tincture. By night seven, Constanze was healthier than she had ever been, and she stayed that way. Ambrose has been trying to repay his debt since that day. Mr. Chan wanted nothing in return and instead pointed Ambrose in a different direction.

LIFE: Ambrose Saloman was born the son of a carpenter and the youngest of three children. By the time he was sixteen, he towered over his brothers and could look his father in the eyes. He took to sports like he took to breathing and his parents were sure that's where his future lay. Everything changed when he heard a fiery violinist attack the opening notes of "Eine kleine Nachtmusik." He worked three jobs to afford his first instrument and continued with two of them to afford lessons. A scholarship allowed him to attend university, the first of his family to do so. He left school and moved to New Paris, Ohio, with a bustling population of 168,000.

The city was like nothing he'd seen before. Dirigibles dotted the sky and steam-powered carriages worked their way through winding streets. Failing to get a position as a music teacher, he busked street corners and played dinner music on airships. Success was eventually his, though he nearly lost everything when Constanze was near death. A golden elixir saved her life where White doctors could not, and he would spend the rest of his life trying to pay back the debt he owed the elderly pharmacist who helped them. It was in this way that Ambrose Saloman became a Rosicrucian and vowed to proclaim only one thing: to heal the sick, and that gratis.

Alchemy, like music, is a lifelong pursuit. In a handful of years, Ambrose became a talented spagyricist, creating medicinal tinctures and elixirs through the alchemy of plants. After many years of labor, Ambrose earned the VII° Adeptus Exemptus and became one of the Chiefs of his Rosicrucian Collage, similar to a Masonic Lodge. Now in his late forties, Brother Ambrose still teaches music and can be found in the back rooms of Mr. Chan's, now his son's, pharmacy, helping those whom the traditional sciences have forsaken. His granddaughter Sophia just entered college to study chemistry and medicine, but also religion and philosophy, and Ambrose carefully followed her carer until she, too, took up the practice of the Royal Art.

AESTHETIC: To the outer world, Ambrose Saloman is a relatively successful private music instructor and is by today's standards solidly middle class, so he dresses the part. Part of the Rosicrucian tradition, stemming directly from the *Fama Fraternitatis,* is to not wear any particular garb and to instead dress as the customs of the land they are in dictates.[266] New Paris, Ohio, is a bustling city of nearly 170,000 souls, and the population has members from all over the world. Fitting in isn't difficult, even for a Black man in late nineteenth-century Ohio.

Ambrose's everyday clothing is just nice enough for him to stand out without sticking out like a sore thumb. His usual ensemble consists of his favorite red bowler hat and a black waistcoat over a white shirt. When teaching, he usually works in shirtsleeves for more freedom of movement; for Ambrose is a passionate player of whatever instrument he holds. Similar to Henry Brougham, Ambrose wears the trappings of his rank and office over his nicer suits, but Lodge clothing is for Lodge, and outside those sacred walls, no one would suspect that Ambrose Saloman was either a Rosicrucian or Alchemist.

DRESSING THE PART: When it comes to "dressing the part," Lodge-based secret societies are tricky. For instance, the only time Freemasons generally wear their aprons and regalia outside of Lodges is in Lodge or Grand Lodge-sanctioned parades or special events such as the laying of a foundation stone. Otherwise, at most, you might see a Masonic ring, or today, a Masonic symbol on the back of someone's car. The point of a secret society, after all, is to be secret. However, we are not without options. For a Rosicrucian alchemist, you can incorporate traditional colors into your ensemble, the most common being the three phases of the alchemical process: black, white, and red. We can see this in Ambrose's clothing.

---

266 See McIntosh 30.

There isn't necessarily any reason to be subtle, though. A red hat and waistcoat will stand out more, and you can add a rose cross lapel pin or, if you wear medals, a rose cross medal that goes with the other ones you wear.

Additionally, if you take the example of a Rosicrucian alchemist, you can lean into the alchemical part of the steamsona. Reagent vials, leather holders, and bandoliers are readily available. With seven, each could be filled with water colored to represent the seven planets. Instead of dressing in just black, white, and red, you can change out a matching cravat or kerchief with one in a planetary color, or even have something embroidered with the symbols of the planets, as seen below:

PLANET	TRADITIONAL COLOR	GOLDEN DAWN COLOR
Sun	Yellow or Gold	Orange
Mercury	Orange or Multicolored	Yellow
Venus	Green	Green
Moon	White or Silver	Blue
Mars	Red	Red
Mars	Blue	Violet
Saturn	Black	Indigo

As astrology is an important part of Western occultism in general, the colors of the planets are more or less appropriate for any of the traditions here discussed, though you will find some variations, such as those used in the Golden Dawn.

THE DRUID

NAME: Dame Eiluned Gwyllt of Caer Annwn
BACKGROUND CONCEPT: Environmentalist in a world of brass
and steam.

Dame Eiluned awakened to her second sight at the age of eleven.
She woke the house screaming in the wee hours of the night.
The sight ran in her family, but the last to have it was Eiluned's
great-grandmother, whom they visited the next day. Over the
course of years, Iola taught her granddaughter the cunning craft
and wise ways. When she died, Eiluned watched her spirit taken
up by a mighty stag, whom she rode into the hollow hills. Eiluned
grew up. College and university followed. By the time she was
twenty-four, she had earned a Master's Degree in environmental
studies. At the age of twenty-five, she inherited the Baronetcy
of Caer Annwn from her mother.

Eiluned's vision remained with her throughout her life. It
was one of a world bereft of nature and instead filled with brass,
iron, and the endless cacophony of machinery. And steam. So
much steam. The world around her could barely be seen. Dame
Eiluned would experience countless other visions during the
course of her life. This, however, would still wake her screaming
in the night. Other visions changed and could be manipulated.
This vision stood immutably before her all her days.

LIFE: Iola Gwalchmai was skilled in the cunning women's
arts, which had been passed down her maternal line from time
immemorial. Eiluned, the most recent descendent of that line,
was less so. She learned to control her visions and was content
to leave the rest to someone else. She had no need for any of
that esoteric nonsense. She instead focused on education, on
language, and on music. She became fluent in Cymraeg before
leaving college and learned to play a handful of instruments,
though she would never become masterful in any of them. That

didn't really matter. The playing, the creating, was more important. She found her way to the gorseddau and wrote poetry and prose, occasionally won a competition with such, and was more or less happy. Then things got worse.

Eiluned's visions became increasingly difficult to control. Sometimes, she could barely tell if what was right in front of her was real or not, and people she had seen in visions suddenly showed up around her. One such person was Mererid. Mererid all but appeared before her at a *gorsedd* as Eiluned wondered the fields around the competition, not entirely certain of the reality around her. But Mererid was *real*, and the world came into focus around her. The older woman drew Eiluned close and wrapped them both in her white cloak. Eiluned didn't find the Henge of the Broken Gear, the Henge had found her.

The path of the Druid was similar in many ways to what Iola had taught her, and yet different in as many more. Dame Eiluned learned the basics of bardcraft before throwing herself at the divinatory work of an *ovydd*. She would master her visionary powers, and with them, roam the world—and even the otherworld—in spirit vision. She learned to read the runes and Ogham and the flight of birds to see past, present, and future. The magic worked by the *derwydds* of the Henge used those visions to change the course of events, the minds of scientists and politicians, and the world. Roads got moved to avoid forests. Mining companies lost permits. Housing developments stalled while the wildlife wreaked havoc on machinery overnight. The vision of a world without nature never leaves her sight, and she doesn't know if it can be forestalled. Despite the Henge's efforts, there was always some great new invention roaring to life every year. But sometimes those inventions made irrigation easier, provided clean water where there was none before, and made an increasingly mechanical world just that much greener. Maybe there was hope after all.

Aesthetic: As a baronetess, society has come to expect certain things of Dame Eiluned, a certain propriety of manner and of dress. Eiluned leans into those expectations hard. Evening gown for a fundraiser? She has a forest green ensemble with oak leaves embroidered on the bodice and silhouettes of falcons flying down her back. Tiny golden sickles adorn her ears. She dances as effortlessly as she draws donations for a new preserve in the moorlands. What's better than a live telectroscope spot in the moorlands to talk about how important they are to preserve? A pair of rugged trousers with a sturdy waistcoat and a hooded overcoat is just the thing. With calf-high leather boots decorated with a carved green man at the cuffs, she stomps over peat and through heather and mud as though she had lived in the moors her entire life. Whatever the public needs her to be, she is there for it, but on her own terms.

Some of her sisters in the Hedge chide Eiluned for making her Druidry that much of her identity. There is always some bit of it about her—an *awen* brooch, the sickle earrings, a motif of flora and fauna practically everywhere about her person. From her view, however, becoming a druid—an *ovydd*—saved her life. In doing so, it became her life. And what does it matter if she is out on the town in a white dress covered by a vest and hooded coat in contrasting shades of the deepest green? People can hardly see her through the steam, anyway.

Dressing the Part: Modern Druidry, Neopagan or otherwise, very much has its own aesthetics. Pictures of white-clad Druids with headdresses and the three-rayed symbol of awen, representing otherworldly inspiration, can readily be found on the internet and in books. The symbol, three spreading rays with a dot above each line, has been attributed to Iolo Morganwg. Fantasy, be it novels, movies, TV, or roleplaying games, also show druids in a variety of ways, with hooded cloaks seeming to be a common thread between them. And, while brown is a steampunk's favorite color, blue, green, and white are colors used to distinguish the three groupings of druids: bard, ovate, and druid. These can be worked in more or less subtly.

Nature—and being out in and a part of it—is a frequent motif. Victorian women were still wearing full skirts and corsets when out hiking, though they would wear boots rather than shoes. Bloomer suits were also becoming popular, and what were originally men's "sport togs," knee breeches with a Norfolk jacket, were becoming popular, and women had been taking men's work clothing for working on the farm for some time already. All of this can, of course, be worked in combination, with a cloak or long coat being worn atop sturdy outdoor wear. Talismans featuring runes from the *Barddas* or Ogham, the *awen,* bits of jewelry with harps, sickles, a triskele or triquetra, as well as Celtic knotwork, can be added to any and all of this. Ogham and runes can also be marked on hats, goggles, and even around the edge of a handkerchief that is tucked into a pocket or sleeve cuff.

THE CUNNING WOMAN

Name: Arabella Bennet
Background Concept: A jack-of-all-trades, more than willing to lend…or rent her knowledge.

Bella had always been a curious person. As a child, she enjoyed nothing more than taking things apart to see how they worked. She even occasionally put them back together again. As she grew up, she learned that those around her valued her knowledge, and some would even pay for it. Where other children spent their pocket money on sweets or bits of ephemeral entertainment, Bella spent her earnings on books and tools and lessons. Anything that was helpful, anything that made her more powerful, anything that made her money was what she was interested in.

Old Jerald began teaching Bella the cunning craft in the middle of her sixteenth year. Her parents—hardworking, industrious folk—had already written her off as a lost cause. No man would want to marry a woman of no means and a smart mouth. As far as they were concerned, Old Jerald could have her. In a year or two, Bella became his full-time apprentice. She booked clients, researched ailments and cures, and she absorbed everything around her. When Jerald died, he left her his library, his tools, and, most importantly, his clients. Bella Bennet knew a spell to make someone fall in love with you in five days and one to make them fall out of love with you in three. She could birth a child or a lamb with equal ease. Need a curse lifted? Is a blight affecting your crops? Everyone knew that Bella would have the answer. And, for a price, it could be yours.

LIFE: Arabella Beatrice Bennet was the youngest of five children and grew up in the port town of New Swanage, Maryland. Her father worked the docks and her mother was a nanny for the brats of the people who owned the company her father worked for. Her siblings were all similarly employed before they were fourteen. Bella would have none of it. She wasn't exactly difficult, but she did have a permanent handmark on her arse for "talking back" so often. She wasn't talking back, exactly—she just had questions. How does this work? Why are we supposed to act this way in public but not in private? If spirits do good things for people, and angels destroy entire cities, why are spirits bad and angels good? Her questions did not make her popular with almost anyone, especially the young men her parents constantly tried to get to marry her. Her sisters were both married on their eighteenth birthdays. Bella had no time for any of that. She saw the lives they lead afterward. They couldn't own property, couldn't vote, couldn't even run the house they were supposedly in charge of. Bella was at a "Votes for Women" rally before the rice had been swept from the church floor after Stella's wedding. By the time Bella was sixteen, she started to be simply called "that girl" around town.

Bella's apprenticeship with Old Jerald lasted years, ending only when he did. She took over everything at that point. Overnight, she transformed from an awkward young woman who should have been married years ago into a master of arcane knowledge; a master who could wither crops with a look or heal anyone who still took breath of whatever disease ailed them. She loved every moment of it. Despite the years she had already spent with Jerald, Bella found that she had barely scratched the tip of the iceberg. She soon found necromancy distasteful, and not particularly useful. She could divine through any number of means and even had a tarot deck made up to her specifications. Her favorite form of divination, though, was geomancy—earth divination. But what really caught her fancy was talismanry. By the end of the summer, she could produce for you a talisman to take care of anything that bothered you.

With her new profession, she also gained something she'd never had before: wealth. While hardly swimming in a pool of gold coins, she no longer had to worry about whether she would become destitute if literally anything went wrong in her life. She bought clothing she liked, had items custom-made, and, for the first time in her life, relaxed. "Miss Bella," as the townsfolks now called her, was welcome almost everywhere. Bella brought with her a treatment for the baker's pregnant wife, a curse of impotence for a cheating husband, a talisman of protection from those idiots in the white hoods, a poultice for the dock worker who gashed their arm while hauling freight. Boon or impediment, wisdom or wit, Arabella Bennet had what you needed, or could get it in short order. For a price.

AESTHETIC: Discretionary income was rather a new thing for Bella Bennet, so one might excuse her if she spent a little excessively when it came to her wardrobe. No longer having to wear third-generation hand-me-downs, she now had clothing custom-made for her. Along with her library and working instruments, clothing was the only thing she really spent money on. Although active in local women's rights groups, she never adopted the "American costume," preferring flowing skirts, tailored blouses, and fitted corsets. The townsfolk politely refer to her style as "eclectic." Bella calls it "witchy chic." Dresses and corsets were often in earth tones, if for no other reason than it hides soil and dirt better than brighter colors. Reagent pouches were always at the ready and hidden pockets in her dresses meant she always had the right tool at hand.

While widely appreciated, Bella is under no illusion that she is universally loved. She isn't the only worker of cures and curses, and someone had to first cast a curse for her to counter. And that impacted other cunning people's—not to mention witches', warlocks', and a host of other practitioners'—businesses. So, she had protective runes carved into the leather of her corsets and decoratively sewn into the cuffs and collars of her blouses. Her flowing dress had psalms embroidered around the hem, with little flowers for accents. This hid the seven-league boots she wore almost everywhere.

DRESSING THE PART: Cunning folk were practical people. Certainly, not all have the wealth Bella does, but this is fiction, so let's go with it. Bella's base clothing is standard, middle-class Victoriana: a blouse and skirt. The bustle is optional because they aren't always practical, but if worn, the smaller bustles would be preferable. External corsets are fairly popular and come in a variety of shapes, sizes, colors, and materials. Pointed witch or wizard hats are always increasingly popular, but there is no reason that you have to go that route. The base clothing can really be just about anything that isn't overly extravagant. Cunning people get their hands dirty, after all.

What sets the cunning person out from others is the accouterments. Cunning people were, and are, part "witch,"[267] part alchemist, part doctor, part herbalist, and part scholar. Bella is shown with leather pouches for herbs and other reagents used for healing. They are marked with Theban script. You could just as well have a bandolier or belt of vials filled with the substances of

---

267 Cunning people generally did not consider themselves to be practitioners of witchcraft. However, their actual practice was often undifferentiable from witchcraft or other forms of folk magic.

your craft. Whereas Dame Eiluned above used traditional colors to define her look, here we are using the artifacts of the craft itself. Wear a bracelet of shields or other talismans, ala Harry Dresden. Mark, carve, or embroider clothing with runes, Theban or other magical scripts, and sigils[268] in contrasting bold colors. Wear the magic, as it were. Make it as subtle or bold as you want.

THE SORCERER

Name: Sèitheach MacGregor, the Steampunk Sorcerer
Background Concept: Curmudgeonly teacher with a heart of…with what we're assuming is a heart.

Sèitheach was born during the reign of James I of Scotland, near Strathmore in northern Scotland, long before the settlements were cleared out in the early part of the 1800s. His parents were shepherds, though the sheep weren't theirs, and supplemented themselves with fishing and hunting. It wasn't a particularly exciting life. His parents died before his sixteenth birthday and with them went the flock to shepherds better able to control the beasts than a single boy. With nothing keeping him, Sèitheach began traveling the highlands. He met the old witch Eilidh in *Mòinteach Raineach*, Rannoch Moor. Trading food for knowledge, Eilidh opened Sèitheach's eyes to a wider, hidden world. He buried her just before Samhain and headed south to Edinburgh, which was still recovering from the English assault. That's where he met sorceress Beathas de Soulis.

This is when Sèitheach considers his life to have really begun. Eilidh taught him how to survive, bewitching animals for easier hunting, finding fresh water, the best fishing spot. Beathas taught him how to thrive. He learned to read and write, not just Scots

---

268 While, generally speaking, such decorations will be just that—decorative—it is still a good idea to know what symbols you are putting on your person. For symbols from grimoires, a fantastic resource is Joseph Peterson's Twilit Grotto: Archives of Western Esoterica website.

but Latin, Greek, and a smattering of Hebrew. He could conjure spirits in their proper hours and bind them to his purpose. He bought nine hundred years of life from the spirit, Aratron. By the time he met Dr. Dee, he was already skilled in the magical arts and had picked up enough accents to sound like he almost belonged in polite society. When he had risen in the Order, they put him in front of a group of novices and told him to teach them something—anything. That's what he did, and hundreds of years later, he continues to do so.

LIFE: Meeting Dee yet again altered the path of Sèitheach's life. He and Beathas had divorced, with Beathas moving to France. Sèitheach became the local sorcerer, enough outside of Edinburgh to be accessible to those in need of his services, but far enough away that it wasn't worth sending people out to arrest him. That had been tried. It didn't turn out well. For them, anyway. He tired of the game after a few decades. Bored, he began traveling Europe. He met Dee, and his young assistant Edward Kelley, in Bohemia in 1585. He turned 174 that October.

Dee filled in the missing parts of Sèitheach's education, both exo- and esoteric. Sèitheach didn't even know what he didn't know. He met Elizabeth I, briefly—very briefly. They didn't get on. He learned to speak with angels, they also didn't get on, and demons. Dee taught him new ways to enchant objects, to skry, to decipher encoded messages, and even a bit of alchemy, though he learned most of what he now knows about it from St. Germain sometime in the 1700s. He was in Germany at the time and only lately heard news of some English colonies making trouble across the sea. Dee brought Sèitheach into the Order of the Ruby Ankh. The Order foisted upon him the job of teaching novices. He took to it like he took polite society—not at all. Over time, he became a real teacher, and over the long years of his life, it remains one of his few passions.

Sèitheach has lived in Glasgow since about 1786, at a part of Lich Street that doesn't exist on any map, and within walking distance of the great necropolis. Having become something resembling respectable, he lectures at the University of Glasgow's Department of Theology and Theoretical Alchemy. With seven-league spats, the Order's Priory in Edinburgh is easily reachable, where he is, lamentably, in charge. Of everything. Having missed a meeting of the Order's governing council, he was made Grand Prior. He does not enjoy the job, but no one else has missed a meeting in the last few hundred years, so he's stuck with it. Whenever his keeper—that is, "secretary"—isn't looking, he still sneaks off to teach the novices things they probably shouldn't know yet.

AESTHETIC: Sèitheach usual attire isn't largely different from anything you might normally encounter in Glasgow or Edinburgh. On most days, he can be found in a grey Argyll Jacket and waistcoat. Sure, he wears a top hat and a pair of spats over his calf-high kilt hose, but usually there is nothing too unusual about them. That is until one takes a closer look. Tarot cards protrude from the crimson hat band and several medals form a row beneath his jacket pocket. These are talismans, and they change out depending on just what is needed; protection, speed in travel, smoothness of speech, or whatever it is he might need. Red embroidery also often graces his seven-league spats, and his cravat is a lamen of the arte. You know, just in case. Not that he doesn't stand out when he wants to. Top hat, wizard's hat, it's all the same; as long as it fulfills its purpose, it doesn't really matter what it is.

When on Order business, a red-lined, hooded cloak, emblazoned with the symbol of his rank of Knight Grand Star simultaneously conceals and reveals his presence. Now in Regulation Doublet or white robes, either his chain of office or the Ruby Ankh lamen adorns his chest. At his side is a scarlet-hilted sword or a walking stick, the top of which glowing crimson. Sèitheach's normally mild demeanor is replaced by one of command and power. Sèitheach MacGregor is a mild-mannered teacher; the Chevalier Sèitheach, GSRA, OT, OHM, is someone else entirely.

Dressing the Part: Most of Sèitheach's clothing is easily attainable and is more or less traditional Scottish attire. Yes, sometimes he'll swap out the standard waistcoat with something a little more extra, but his clothing is largely available through retail. There are some exceptions. A waistcoat was hand embroidered and the spats, cravat, and black hooded cloak were custom-made and embroidered with symbols from the Greater Key of Solomon and the Order of the Ruby Ankh.

The medals are a bit more difficult. One is a pin I had custom-made and will occasionally give out while at conventions. The other I usually wear came from an online retailer. There are a few others that I occasionally switch out, which again came from online retailers. The leather top hat always has three tarot cards in the hat band, which are photocopies rather than cards from the actual deck. Sometimes I wear a large leather wizard's hat instead—because I can. While out and about, I might play Sèitheach rather subtly with fewer accouterments, but at a con, the point is to be visible and fun—and maybe just a little intimidating.

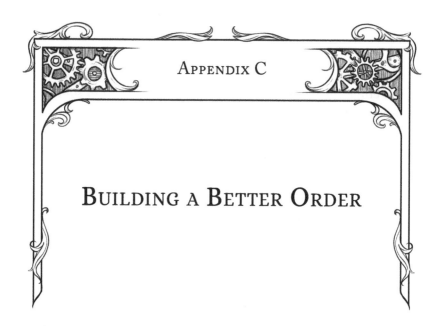

APPENDIX C

BUILDING A BETTER ORDER

It is entirely possible for your steamsona to be a member of an extant, or even defunct but historical, esoteric organization, but there isn't necessarily a good reason to do so. While some organizations, such as the Golden Dawn, have a certain amount of name recognition, they may also have a certain amount of infamy that you might not want to deal with. A lot of orders were also quite racist, which is something we should not like to be associated with. Also, when you've attached yourself to something that actually existed, there comes with it an expectation that you know enough about it to fake it properly. I've provided you with the bare bones of histories and personalities, but your steamsona should have some meat to it. In this lies the advantage of creating your own fictional organization. The Order of the Ruby Ankh, mentioned above, is an example of someone having done exactly that.[269]

The preceding chapters should help you get a feel for what sort of things occult organizations, orders, groves, circles, temples, and what have you do, how they operate, and how they might

---

269 Me. I'm someone.

look. For instance, almost anything connected to Freemasonry has at the very least a three-degree system. We see such degree systems in Martinism, the Golden Dawn, the OTO, and Wicca in its initiatory forms. Something more druidic will likely have divisions between bards, ovates, and druids, potentially with subdivisions within those three orders.

Your order should also have some uniquely identifying regalia or clothing; the masonic apron, the grade sash, the cord of initiation, colored robes, or the "American costume" from Spiritualism. Other aspects of their material culture might include medals, talismans, the use of special alphabets on their garb, magical notebooks, and other such tomes. You can call yourself by whatever title you might like, whether it is Frater, Maestro, Worshipful Master, Sir or Dame Knight, or something else to your liking. The advantage of creating your own fictional organization, even if you are effectively its only member, is that it is yours. You can do whatever you'd like with it and there really is no one to challenge you on its historical accuracy outside of blatant anachronism. Even that can be easily written off as something that exists at that time in the steampunk world you inhabit, even if it didn't exist in ours. This is how the Order of the Ruby Ankh began.

Create a history. It can be as outrageous as you'd like. I'm not aware of any Victorian occult society that didn't lie about how it came about. Chartered by Rosicrucians with lineage going back to CRC himself? Go for it. Contacted by Secret Masters who provide your group with all its wisdom? That's been done, so feel free.[270] The last surviving rite stemming from Greco-Egyptian Alexandria? You'd likely be neither the first nor the last of those. An ancient order of knights? Be my guest. While you may wish to stay away from are things discussed above in the "Don't Expand the Empire!" section, feel free to explore anything else. Fill out the history as much or as little as you like. You may

---

270 Maybe don't make them pseudo-Indian.

find that some things need to be altered or expanded upon. You may find that some things simply don't work. Just drop those elements. Victorian occult societies were just as likely to change their histories as they were to make them up in the first place.

The Order of the Ruby Ankh, ORCA, came about more or less at the same time as Sèitheach did. He, and it, were largely created for me to be more comfortable around large groups of people I didn't know. I'm fairly introverted. Sèitheach, not so much. For a panel on the summoning of spirits, I created a ritual framework that was supposed to be a one-off demonstration, and somehow it stuck. This ended up meaning I had to create a larger framework, as other people became interested in playing along.

The Order became an order of knighthood rather than a more typical fraternal society. There wasn't a particular reason for this, it just sounded nifty. It also gave me an excuse when someone asked about whatever medals I might have been wearing. The Order has three ranks, drawing from the three-degree system mentioned above: Knight, Knight Commander, and Knight Grand Star. These are based on the ranks found in modern orders of knighthood such as the Order of the Garter. Technically, there is also an Associate degree, rather like the 0° that some orders have. In ORCA, an Associate is not yet a knight, but generally just hangs out with us and might be interested in getting more involved in the panels and presentations we do. All knights, regardless of rank or gender, are referred to as Chevalier, which is common amongst European orders rather than the English use of "Sir" or "Dame."

Continuing the theme of European honorary orders of knighthood, the main garb is a cloak emblazoned with the full symbol of the Order. The coloring of both the symbol and the lining of the hooded cloaks depends on the rank of the knight and follows alchemical symbolism. ORCA's pseudo-history does make it clear that it was, and continues to be, a functional order of knighthood rather than merely an honorary one. Why? Again, because it sounded nifty. What battles were we involved in? I'm sorry, but that is above your degree.

We have put on rituals, knighting ceremonies, and numerous panels on occult topics, simultaneously acting as relative authorities on the subjects that we present and a self-parody of Victorian occult orders, which, quite frankly, were often ridiculous. Which is to say, we take our subject seriously, but not ourselves.

This is only one of a myriad of possibilities for how your own order, society, coven, or however else you wish to style it, might look. Find the things you like and build on those. Don't like alchemical symbolism? Astrology has all sorts of imagery to borrow from. Like elements of Druidry but want the aesthetics of steampunk technology? Technopaganism is a thing. Add what you like, remove what you don't, but, most importantly, make it yours and have fun.

Appendix D

Magical Alphabets

Below are presented the five alphabets that have been mentioned throughout the book. Of these, Coelbren y Beirdd from the *Barddas* is the only one that is truly modern, though technically Theban, first appearing in 1518, is from the early Modern period. The rest, though old, are not necessarily ancient; with the earliest examples of all of them coming from the Common Era. Examples such as the Elder Futhark are first seen around the third century CE, and Younger Futhark to the seventh and eighth centuries. Examples of Ogham date to as early as the fourth century CE. Of all these, only Ogham and the runes originate as the written forms of living languages. The runes were, and continue to be, used on both monuments, which were often decorated with various dragons, gods, or other such beings, and on the page, ogham shows up on stone monuments. Theban was used as a simple replacement cipher and is still typically used as such. Coelbren y Beirdd had similar, but also magical, uses. Evidence of the Futhark and Ogham being used for divinatory purposes, as they are today, is relatively modern.

OGHAM

AICME BEITHE

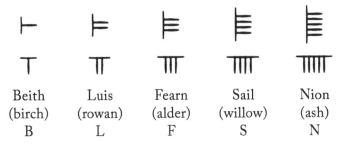

Beith (birch) B	Luis (rowan) L	Fearn (alder) F	Sail (willow) S	Nion (ash) N

AICME HÚATHA

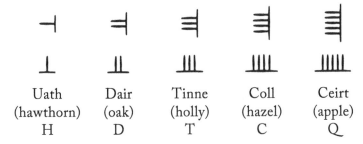

Uath (hawthorn) H	Dair (oak) D	Tinne (holly) T	Coll (hazel) C	Ceirt (apple) Q

AICME MUINE

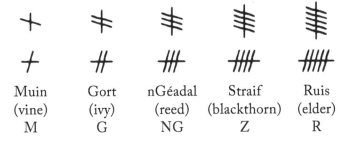

Muin (vine) M	Gort (ivy) G	nGéadal (reed) NG	Straif (blackthorn) Z	Ruis (elder) R

AICME AILME

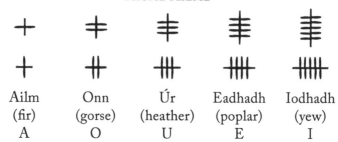

Ailm	Onn	Úr	Eadhadh	Iodhadh
(fir)	(gorse)	(heather)	(poplar)	(yew)
A	O	U	E	I

AICME FORFEDA

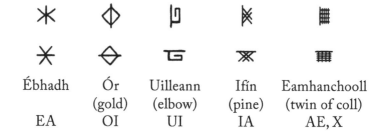

Ébhadh	Ór	Uilleann	Ifín	Eamhanchooll
	(gold)	(elbow)	(pine)	(twin of coll)
EA	OI	UI	IA	AE, X

Adare Stone
County Limerick

ELDER FUTHARK

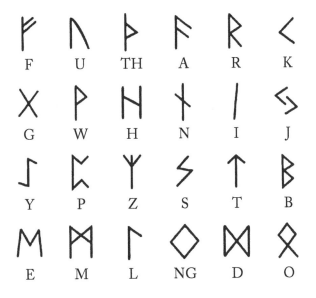

F	U	TH	A	R	K
G	W	H	N	I	J
Y	P	Z	S	T	B
E	M	L	NG	D	O

YOUNGER FUTHARK

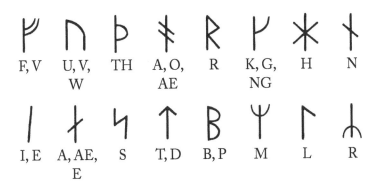

F, V	U, V, W	TH	A, O, AE	R	K, G, NG	H	N
I, E	A, AE, E	S	T, D	B, P	M	L	R

COELBREN Y BEIRDD

Λ	Λ	⅃	⅃	|	Y
A	Â	E	Ê	I	U
1	2			3	

Ψ	Y	◇	◈	V	V
Û	Y	O	Ô	W	Ŵ
		4			

L	ⴿ	W	ⴽ	Ⴑ	Γ	N
B, BI	M	M, MI	V	V	P, PI	PH
5		6			7	

ⴼ	F	<	K	ⴷ	ⴻ	♢
MH	F, FI	C, CI	CH	NGH	G	NG
	8	9			10	

↑	ⴕ	Ⴖ	>	▷	Ⱅ	Ⱅ
T	TH	NH	D, DI	DH	N	N, NI
11			12			13

Ⱔ	N	Ⲅ	Ⲇ	Ⲓ	Ⴞ	Ⲅ
L, LI	LL	R, RI	RH	S, IS	H	HW
14		15		16		

156

THEBAN

A	B	C	D	E	F	G	H

I,J	K	L	M	N	O	P	Q

R	S	T	U,V,W	X	Y	Z	.

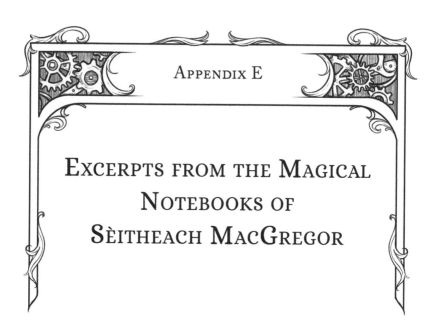

Excerpts from the Magical Notebooks of Sèitheach MacGregor

Steampunks tend to have a lot of props. Vials on a bandolier filled with unknown substances, mechanical arms, strange tools to work on one's airship, and any number of things that light up, spin, smoke, steam, or otherwise go *whirr* in the day. There is no reason your occultist steamsona can't have that too. One thing that seems to have been common amongst ceremonial magicians of this era, especially those coming from some variation of the Golden Dawn or its offshoots, is the magical notebook.

These would have originally been hand-copied versions of the grade material the magician was expected to learn. These would eventually become largely typewritten, with hand-drawn diagrams usually in black and red. The Golden Dawn encouraged the student to not put all the material in a single notebook, so if it was found by someone outside the Order, only that small amount of material would fall into their hands. Wicca seemingly borrowed from this concept in the development of the Book of Shadows. This is a handwritten tome, often done in calligraphy or other ornate penmanship, that contains all of a Wiccan's rituals, lore, and other teachings—or anything else they might find relevant to their Craft.

Your notebook, notebooks, or oversized spell tome can be a simple affair (as are most of what we have from various Golden Dawn collections), hand bound, or even feature embossed leather covers. Hand-binding books is not terribly difficult, and there are a number of different styles with which to stitch the signatures. Some of these, such as Coptic binding and Japanese stab binding, are also quite decorative. Fully binding and covering a book requires, or is at least much easier with, some specialized equipment, such as a book press and a sewing frame. Much of this can be made if you have a drill, wood bits, and a bit of free time. I have made both the items mentioned above and by no means am I a skilled worker in wood.

Admittedly, notebooks are not necessarily the sexiest prop to carry around. Certainly, you can make it look as fancy as possible, for instance, with brightly colored thread for stitching the signatures and a contrasting cover. Or, as mentioned above, the larger Magical Tome™ bound in leather and embossed with the symbols of your order, coven, or grove. The latter can be attached to leather straps and worn on your back for everyone to see. The former could be holstered, rather like the teacup holsters that are quite popular amongst steampunks. You can also make or buy a pouch, again with all the appropriate symbols on it, to carry the notebooks in. This has the advantage of letting you carry things with your hands free and you get two props instead of just the notebook.

The notebook or Magical Tome™ doesn't need to have anything actually written in it, with the cover or stitching or other decorations being the main part of the prop. Having at least a handful of pages with some sort of content, even if it isn't anything more than "lorem ipsum" in a typewriter font and some drawings, adds some mystique and flair. What follows are "excerpts" from one of the magical notebooks of the Chevalier Sèitheach MacGregor. This is just an example of what sort of things one might put in their notebooks. You will see that, although inscribed in a typewritten style, special characters or images are drawn in. We have several examples of this in Golden Dawn notebooks, with Hebrew and Greek being handwritten in an otherwise typed book.

The cover page of this notebook is a good example of this. Commercially available typewriters became available in 1863 and would not have been able to accommodate differently sized typefaces, let alone other alphabets. If something needed to be larger or smaller than what the typewriter could produce, it would have to be handwritten. As much of the cover page is like that, the entirety of it has been hand-drawn.

$$2° = \text{☿}°$$

Knight Commander

∴O∴R∴C∴A∴

Book of Rituals

Consisting of the Foundational Rites of the
Ordo Rubeus Crux Ansata
with Explanations

Cyprianus House

Glasgow Priory

1897

(1)

THE BANISHMENT of the
FLAMING SWORD of PROMETHEVS

The Banishing of the Flaming Sword of Prometheus is to be employed for general protection. This ritual is to be used before and after any working, regardless of its nature. The Banishment consists of four steps.

The Invocation of the Depths

1. After several moments of relaxation, stand in the centre of the Priory, facing East. If you have a central altar, stand just to the West of it. Imagine around your body your imagio or aura. See it as being made of iridescent flames rising from your feet and surrounding your body in an ovoid shape. The flames become the most brilliant above the crown of your head. Hold this image for several moments.
2. Clasp your hands over your heart. If you are holding an implement to trace the seals with, hold it between your clasped hands pointing downward.
3. Intone the words AB INITIO AD FINEM. Visualise a beam of soft white illuminating your imagio, stretching between your right and left shoulders.
4. Intone the words DE BONO AD MALVM. Visualise a beam of soft white light illuminating your imagio from above to below. The beams should cross at your heart centre.
5. Intone the words A DEO OMNIA. AMEN. As you do this, feel the light from your heart centre expanding and merging into your imagio. As the light from both within and without merge, know that the light from without is the Light of your own higher Mens.

(2)

Wielding the Flaming Sword

1. Move to the East and draw the Flaming Sword in the air before you, from sky to ground, while intoning DEVS.
2. Still pointing towards the ground, trace the perimeter of your circle while moving to the South.
3. Draw the Flaming Sword as before. Intone IMMORTALIS.
4. Still pointing towards the ground, trace the perimeter of your circle while moving to the West.
5. Draw the Flaming Sword as before. Intone POTENS.
6. Still pointing towards the ground, trace the perimeter of your circle while moving to the North.
7. Draw the Flaming Sword as before. Intone IN AETERNVM.
8. Trace the perimeter to the East, completing the circle.

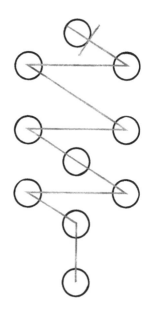

(3)

The Invocation of the Princes

1. Stand in the Sign of the Ankh.
2. Say the following, intoning the Names of the Princes:

'In the name of the Highest:
On my right hand: AVSTER
On my left hand: AQVILO
Before me: VULTVRNVS
Behind me: FAVONIVS
And above my head, mighty CAELVM
Below my feet, stalwart TELLVS
And within the center of all things is
mighty SATVRNVS.'

3. Clasp your hands over your heart. If you are holding an implement to trace the seals with, hold it between your clasped hands pointing downward.
4. To finish, perform the Invocation of the Depths.

EXPLANATION

The Banishment begins and ends with the invocation of the depths. First, the depths of Beginning and End are invoked with 'Ab Initio Ad Finem', which means 'From Beginning to End'. This defines the temporal region of creation, but in a spiritualized form. It is beginning and end, the Alpha et Omega of Christianity, but it is also, and eternally, the now.

The temporal aspect of creation is then followed by the moral aspect, 'De Bono Ad Malum', or 'From Good to Evil'. This brings down the Divine Light from the highest sources beyond manifestation into the moral world that we live in. This follows the temporal calling

of beginning and end as morality exists through one's deeds, and there can be no action without time.

The calling of these four spiritual depths serves to attach Above to Below. The Divine Light is then, and finally, brought forth into manifestation through the invocation of Godhead: A Deo Omnia, meaning 'Everything comes from God'. This is finally sealed with 'Amen'. Thus is the Light bound into the imagio of the Knight, who in turn strives towards becoming a being and emissary of Light for the benefit and protection of the world.

The Sign of the Flaming Sword is then drawn in the four quarters. This Sword is a combination of Mercury's adamantine sword and the fire Prometheus brought from the heavens. The Sword is given power through the invocation of the divine 'Deus Immortalis Potens ad Aeturnum', or 'Immortal God is Mighty Forever'. This phrase invokes the powers of the four elements in the lower world, as well as at the Realm of Creation known as the 'lower astral', which exists directly above, ontologically speaking, our own Realm of Action, which includes the gross physical world and the 'etheric' plane.

Last is the invocation of the Princes of Air, the Four Winds, as well as the height and ground of all things, the Heavens and Earth. The Princes are called in their traditional directions, which also correspond to the four elements. Above all things is invoked the Heavens, Caelum, or Ouranos. Below is the Earth itself, Tellus, Terra, or Gaia, who is both the mother and wife of Caelum. Standing in the center, the same place as the Knight is mighty Saturnus, who established a Golden Age of peace and harmony. Together, these are the guardian and establishing forces of the universe.

(5)

Finally, as we began so do we end, with the Invocation of the Divine Light through the Depths. We once again establish the Light within ourselves and the created universe around us.

THE RITUAL of the RUBY ANKH

The Ruby Ankh is a powerful symbol representing the operation of the Tetrad of Life throughout creation and is used to invoke all Powers, generative, psychic, celestial, and supercelestial. The Ankh is the Signet of the Lady of Life, and so do we call upon that Lady before any operation of the Ritual of the Ruby Ankh. Thus, we proclaim: 'Per ná ám repa Aset'! 'I come forth therefrom into the House of Aset'! Because it is symbolic of the Power of Life itself, it is to be employed whenever a Power is to be vivified into action, or when it is necessary for that action to halt or be banished.

Call not upon the powers Divine for any whim or fancy, but only with solemnity and purpose. These demiurgic forces of the Cosmoses, who are the Creative Powers set above all things, demand the greatest purity of mind and consecration of heart. Such gnosis can only be received by the Knight whose purified soul and illuminated Mind can stand before the dazzling Brilliance of the Craftsman who sits at the feet of the One Beyond All Things. Beneath the Creators are a myriad of powers and potentates and these may be called upon, but always with due respect and caution.

When drawing the Symbol of a Planet in the centre of an Ankh, it is to be made proportionate to the superior sphere of the Ankh. Draw all such Symbols as you have been taught, moving sunwise to invoke, and counter to banish. To invoke or banish the power

(6)

of Divine Life, the Ankh is drawn towards the proper place, and seen with the Spirit Vision as formed from a brilliant Ruby. The Signs may be Seen in brilliant white light.

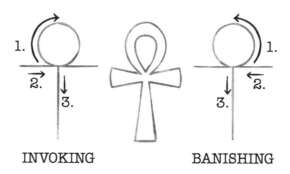

INVOKING   BANISHING

Due to the movements of both Earth and the Sky above, in order to call upon or banish the powers of the planets or zodiac, it is necessary to cast a chart of the sky for the precise time and place of the working to know the location of the heavenly bodies. A plaque representing the Planet(s) and/or Sign(s) should be set in the place of the Planet or Sign as found in the astrological chart.

Alternatively, an idealized map of the Heavens may be erected within the Priory. For this, place a plaque representing Aries directly to the East and at the border of the circle. Place plaques of the remaining Signs evenly spaced around the circumference of the Priory. The Planetary powers may be invoked or banished by placing a plaque of one or more Planets before the Signs, either in their place at the time of the working, to transform the Priory into an astrological chart most favorable to your intent.

(7)

In all Rituals of the Ruby Ankh, the Knight shall complete the circle of the place with the Banishment of the Flames of Prometheus. An external circle is not to be drawn around each Ankh or sigil unless the powers invoked are to be concentrated into a single place, such as in the consecration of a Talisman or Weapon of the Arte.

The power of the Ruby Ankh may be called upon in its invoking or banishing form. When working with supercelestial Powers, the Name AEON is intoned as the Ankh is drawn. When working with heavenly Powers, the name SOLIS is intoned as the Ankh is drawn. When working with powers of the World Soul, the name ANIMA is intoned as the Ankh is drawn. When working with generative Powers, the Name SALVATOR is intoned as the Ankh is drawn.

THE NAMES of the COSMOSES

COSMOS	DIVINITY	NAME
Supercelestial Realm	AEON (Eternity)	COGITAMENTA (Thoughts)
Celestial Realm	SOLIS (Of the Sun)	MENS (Mind)
Psychic Realm	ANIMA (Soul)	VITA (Life)
Generative Realm	SALVATOR (Savior)	IMAGO (Image)

(8)

In order to call upon or banish the Heavenly Powers of the Planets, the Divine Name of the planet is intoned while pointing to the Ankh's opening. In order to call upon or banish the Celestial Powers of the Planets, the sigil of the planet is drawn in the Ankh's opening while its divine name is intoned:

THE PLANETARY POWERS

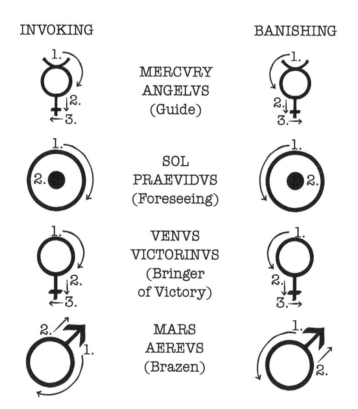

INVOKING		BANISHING
	MERCVRY ANGELVS (Guide)	
	SOL PRAEVIDVS (Foreseeing)	
	VENVS VICTORINVS (Bringer of Victory)	
	MARS AEREVS (Brazen)	

(9)

INVOKING   BANISHING

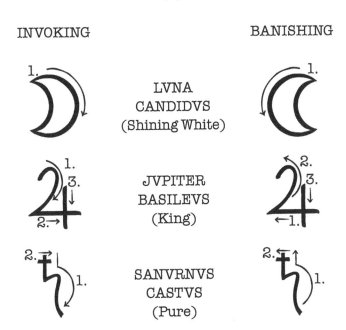

LVNA
CANDIDVS
(Shining White)

JVPITER
BASILEVS
(King)

SANVRNVS
CASTVS
(Pure)

The powers of the Zodiac are called through the Names of their ruling, with the Zodiacal sign used instead of the Planetary. The drawing of all signs should be generally clockwise to invoke and anti-clockwise to banish.

THE ZODIACAL POWERS

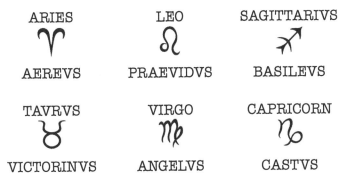

ARIES

AEREVS

LEO

PRAEVIDVS

SAGITTARIVS

BASILEVS

TAVRVS

VICTORINVS

VIRGO

ANGELVS

CAPRICORN

CASTVS

(10)

GEMINI	LIBRA	AQVARIVS
ANGELVS	CANDIDVS	CASTVS
CANCER	SCORPIO	PISCES
CANDIDVS	AEREVS	BASILEVS

In order to call upon or banish the Generative Powers of the Elements, the sigil of the Element is drawn in the Ankh's opening while its divine name is intoned:

THE ELEMENTAL POWERS

SPIRIT

CVSTODES SPIRITVS

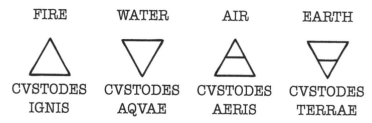

FIRE	WATER	AIR	EARTH
CVSTODES IGNIS	CVSTODES AQVAE	CVSTODES AERIS	CVSTODES TERRAE

There are two primary forms of the Ritual of the Ruby Ankh: The Planar Ritual of the Ruby Ankh and the Supreme Ritual of the Ruby Ankh. The Planar

(11)

Ritual is used to invoke or banish the powers of one of the Five Neoplatonic Cosmoses. This is especially useful when engaging in the practice of Rising Upon the Planes. The Greater Ritual is employed to invoke or banish one or more powers: elemental, planetary, zodiacal, and/or divine.

All forms of the Ritual begin with the Invocation of the Depths and end with the Gesture of the Ogdoad, thus:

The Gesture of the Ogdoad

1. Hold your arms before you, bent at the elbows and parallel to the floor. The palms should face each other. Say: 'The chaos from which eternity blossoms'.
2. Touch palms together and slide your hands down your arms until you can grasp fingers. Say: 'The eternity from which darkness is conceived'.
3. Bow your head and cover your eyes with the palms of your hands. Say: 'The darkness from which air is begot'.
4. Raise your head and lower your arms, palms up, until they are parallel with the floor. Say: 'The breath of life'.

THE PLANAR RITUAL of the RUBY ANKH

1. Proclaim: 'Per ná ám repa Aset'!
2. Perform the Invocation of the Depths.
3. Draw the invoking or banishing Ankhs in the four quarters of the circle. Intone the proper Names while drawing the Ankhs.

(12)

4. Draw the circle on the ground as in the Banishment of the Flame of Prometheus. Complete the circle in the East after the fourth Ankh is drawn.
5. Return to the centre of the Priory. Draw a final invoking or banishing Ankh towards the East while intoning the divine and then the esoteric Name of the World, which is then written in the centre of the Ankh.
6. Perform the Invocation of the Princes.
7. Perform the Invocation of the Depths.
8. Perform the Gesture of the Ogdoad.

THE SUPREME RITUAL of the RUBY ANKH

1. Proclaim: 'Per ná ám repa Aset'!
2. Perform the Invocation of the Depths.
3. Draw the invoking or banishing Ankhs of the Power involved in the four quarters of the circle. Within each Ankh, draw the Sign of the power being invoked or banished while intoning the proper divine Name.
4. Draw the circle on the ground as in the Banishment of the Flames of Prometheus. Complete the circle in the East after the fourth Ankh is drawn.
5. Return to the centre of the Priory. Stand so the altar is between yourself and the position of the element, planet, or sign with which you are working. Draw a final invoking or banishing Ankh with proper Sign and Names in the direction of the planet or sign. If working with the supercelestial heavenly powers, stand West of the altar, facing East, and draw the Signs over the altar and intone the Name as usual.

(13)

6. Repeat this for all Powers invoked or banished.
7. Perform the Invocation of the Princes.
8. Perform the Invocation of the Depths.
9. Perform the Gesture of the Ogdoad.

THE OPENING of the PENTAD

1. Perform the Invocation of the Depths

The Formulation of the Pentad

1. Imagine a corona of flames condensing to form a sphere of white flame, about a handspan across, just above the crown of your head. This is the Caelum centre. Intone the Name DEVS.
2. From the Caelum, see a beam of light rushing forth in one ray down to your throat. This is the gate of gnosis, the Scientia centre. Visualise a sphere of white flame about a hand-span across and intone AMOR.
3. From Scientia, see a beam of white light rushing forth in one ray to your chest; this is the Cor centre. There, visualise a sphere of white flame about a hand-span across and intone SOPHIA.
4. From the Cor, see a beam of white light rushing forth in one ray down to your groin; this is the Radix centre. Visualise there a sphere of white flame about a hand-span across and intone POTENS.
5. From Radix, see a beam of white light rushing forth in one ray down to between your feet; this is the Thronus centre. Visualise there a sphere of white flame about a hand-span across, half above the floor and half beneath. Intone the Name DOMINVS.

(14)

The Formulation of the Wings of Life

1. Begin rhythmic breathing. Inhale to a count of five and visualise white light spiraling clockwise upwards from Thronus to Cor.
2. Hold your breath for a count of four and see the pillar of light between the centres, as well as Thronus, Cor, and Caelum, becoming stronger.
3. Exhale to a count of five and visualise that light concentrated in Cor streaming out your back in the form of two great, upward-reaching wings of light.
4. Hold your breath for a count of four and see the pillar of light between the centres, as well as Thronus, Cor, and Caelum, becoming stronger.
5. Inhale to a count of five and visualise white light spiraling down, anti-clockwise, from Caelum to Cor.
6. Hold your breath for a count of four and see the pillar of light between the centres, as well as Thronus, Cor, and Caelum, becoming stronger.
7. Exhale to a count of five and visualise that light concentrated in Cor streaming out your back in the form of two great, downward-reaching wings of light.

The Rousing of the Body of Flame

1. See the five Pentad from Caelum to Thronus complete and brightly glowing as spheres of pure white flame. Visualise on your right side a pillar of gold rising to the height of your shoulders. On your left, visualise a pillar of silver of the same height. Between these, see a great pillar of copper rising to the height of the top of your head. Each glowing centre should reside within this central pillar.

(15)

2. Visualise all the heavenly fire you have generated through the Pentad as iridescent emerald-green flames. Send this fire to Thronus. Begin rhythmic breathing as before. Inhale and visualise this light moving up the centre of your body to Cor, twisting together clockwise as three tongues of flame. Keep the flames at Cor while holding your breath. Exhale and send the fire back to Thronus, moving it down the sides of your body, along the gold and silver pillars. Repeat this process three, six, or nine times.

3. Bring the fire to Caelum, raising it up the two pillars at your sides. Let the flame rest there as vibrant emerald fire. Inhale and bring the fire down to Cor in a clockwise spiraling triple-flame. Exhale and send the fire back to Caelum, moving up along the gold and silver pillars. Repeat this process the same number of times as in step two. Bring the flame to rest at Caelum.

4. Still breathing rhythmically, inhale and push the fire down to Cor in a tight triple spiral. Hold the fire there as you hold your breath. Exhale and send the emerald flame to Thronus in a burst, seeing it explode from there and rising in flaming glory around your imago. The explosive fire should cause the flames to rise along your imago back to Caelum, where you will once again collect it. All of this occurs during the exhalation. Repeat as above. Bring the flame to rest at Thronus.

5. Again, raise the fire up the centre of your body to Cor while inhaling. Hold the flame there as you hold your breath, and as you exhale send the flame to rise up and burst forth from Caelum. Visualise the iridescent flames spilling down the ovoid shape of your imago and gathering again at Thronus. Repeat as above.

(16)

6. Finally, with the fire in Thronus, inhale and bring it up the centre of your body to Cor. Hold and then exhale the fire out to your imago.

Dismissing the Imago and the Spiritual Depths

1. See the fire expelled from Cor enflaming your imago once again. Allow this image to stay in your mind's eye for a while. When ready, allow the fire to recede until they vanish from your imagination. Know that they still exist and can be recalled as necessary.
2. After several moments of holding this image in your mind's eye, clasp your hand over Cor.
3. Finish by performing the Invocation of the Depths.

Notes

Repeated practise of the Opening of the Pentad has several benefits. Most importantly, it teaches the Knight to control their personal energy. Second, it introduces the Knight to the Divine Names on a personal level, allowing for an experience of the Divine Light directly and as a bolster to their personal energy. Third, much like the Banishment of the Flames of Prometheus, the Opening of the Pentad will, over time, strengthen and seal the Knight's imago to external influences.

The first point of the rite proper, excluding the Invocation of the Depths, employs five centres along the middle pillar of the body. It is important to practise the Opening of the Pentad regularly and to become proficient in it. Later ritual work will build directly upon this rite, and failure to gain proficiency will bar the way towards the higher grades. Further, regular practice strengthens the imago and serves to purify it, thus working to develop

(17)

your magical personality and so bringing yourself more in tune with your 'Mens', the higher mind.

The second point of the rite involves the creation of four angelic wings extending from Cor at your back. The wings connect the Above and the Below within the Knight's imago. Specifically, the wings connect the Intellective and Generative Realms at the point of the Psychic Realm within the Knight.

The final point of the rite is the Rousing of the Body of Flame. The Rousing energizes the imago, bathing it in Divine fire. The Three-Fold Formula used for projecting power is based upon this stage. The rite begins and ends by the Invocation of the Depths.

This rite must be practised regularly in order for the Knight to reap its benefits. Towards this end, it is recommended that the exercise be approached in a number of stages:

1. Visualise the sphere of fire only in white and intone each Name only once. This should be done for a minimum of three weeks before proceeding. The Wings of Life should be performed no more than four times in a single exercise.
2. Second, visualise the Pentad in their appropriate colours (see below). The fire in the Rousing of the Body of Flame should also be seen in colour, corresponding to the fire's location during the exercise. This should be done for a minimum of four weeks before proceeding.
3. Intone each name three times rather than once. This should be done for a minimum of two months before proceeding.
4. Utilise the complete Three-Fold Formula with each Name.

(18)

COLOURS of the PENTAD

CENTRES	COLOURS
Caelum	Brilliance
Scientiam	Light Green
Cor	Citron Green
Radix	Orange
Thronus	Indigo

The Pentad
The Three Pillars
The Wings of Life

(19)

THE THREE-FOLD FORMULA

<u>Adorned Rendition</u>

1. Stand straight with your arms at your sides. Visualise your imago with iridescent flames rising from Thronus and surrounding your body in an ovoid shape, with the flames becoming the most brilliant at the crown of your head.
2. Visualise this corona of flames condensing to form a sphere of white light, about a hand-span in diameter, at Caelum. Concentrate your inner vision on this sphere of white light, seeing it strongly filled with great radiance, and burning with iridescent white flames.
3. Inhale and visualise the Name to be intoned and projected written in this brilliantly white sphere. The Name should be seen as written in black fire.
4. Exhale, visualising a beam of white light rushing forth in one ray from Caelum to Thronus. See Thronus as glowing with an impenetrable darkness burning with iridescent black flames. See the Name written there in white fire.
5. Inhale and visualise a reflux of green flame rising from Thronus to Cor. Cor should be seen as burning with citron-green flames. Visualise the Name written there in violet fire.
6. Exhale. Hold the fire and the Name in Cor.
7. Repeat steps three (3) through six (6) three times, or as many times as there are letters in the Name.
8. Inhale. Make the first part of the Sign of Glory, with your hands, palms in, on either side of Cor.

(20)

9. Exhale. Thrust the Name at Cor up your arms and out through your fingers and eyes towards the object of the projection while simultaneously intoning the Name. Visualise rays of white, fiery light converging upon the point of your projection. To cease the projection, stomp with your left foot, the left representing the side of severity and withholding.

10. Repeat steps one (1) through six (6).

11. Inhale. Concentrate on the citron-green flames of Cor and let the other centres fade from consciousness.

12. Exhale and send the power of Cor into your imago until the ovoid form is filled with flaming power. Let the image of the flaming imago fade from view.

<u>Simple Rendition</u>

1. Inhale. See the Name to be intoned written in black flames in Caelum.

2. Exhale and send the Name, still in black flames, to Thronus in a ray of white light.

3. Inhale and bring the Name of black flames to Cor in a ray of white light.

4. Thrust the Name at Cor up your arms and out through your fingers and eyes towards the object of the projection while simultaneously intoning the Name. Visualise rays of white, fiery light converging upon the point of your projection. To cease the projection, stomp with your left foot, the side of severity and withholding.

(21)

THE POWERS of the COSMOSES

	SUPERCELESTIAL	CELESTIAL
Empyreus	AEON	SOLIS
Primum Mobile	CAELVS	METATRVN
Stellae Fixae	PROVIDENTIAE	VOLVNTAS DEI
Saturnus	CASTVS	SCIENTIA DEI
Jupiter	BASILEVS	IVSTITIA DEI
Mars	AERVS	CALORIX DEI
Sol	PRAEVIDVS	MENDICVS DEI
Venus	VICTORINVS	GRATIA DIE
Mercurius	ANGELVS	QVIS VT DEVS
Luna	CANDIDVS	FORTITVDO DEI
Ignis	MVLCIBER	ARDERE
Aer	LVCINA	LEO DEI
Aqua	TVTVS	SMARAGDOS
Terra	VIRIDIS	BENEDICERE

	PSYCHIC	PSYCHIC	GENERATIVE
Empyreus	ANIMA	(Hosts)	SALVATOR
Primum Mobile	PRIMVM DEI	Seraphs	IGNIS DEI
Stellæ Fixæ	FVNDAMEN-TVM DEI	Kerubs	BENEDICTIO DEI
Saturnus	CELERITAS DEI	Throni	THRONVS DEI
Jupiter	TEGVMEN-TVM DEI	Dominationes	DOMINIVM DEI
Mars	VENENVM DEI	Copiae	VIRTVS DEI

(22)

	PSYCHIC	PSYCHIC	GENERATIVE
Sol	QVIS VT DEVS	Potestates	POTENTIA DEI
Venus	VENVSTAS DEI	Principatus	PRINCIPAT-VM DEI
Mercurius	MENDICVS DEI	Archangelus	SVPERNVN-TIS DEI
Luna	FORTITVDO DEI	Angelus	NVNTIS DEI
Ignis	POSSIDERE DEI	Salamandrae	DJIN
Aer	AUDENS DEI	Sylphae	PARALDA
Aqua	ROS DEI	Undine	NIKSA
Terra	TAVRVS DEI	Gnomai	GHOB

EVOCATION of the
ELYMPIC PLANETARY SPIRIT OPHIEL

In the Antechamber:

The Robe   The Sword of the Arte
The Lamen   The Laver of Lustral Water
The Cloak of your Rank A white towel
and Grade

In the Priory:

The Magic Circle   The Ruby Ankh
The Triangle of the   The Chalice and
Arte, placed in the   Lustral Water
direction of Mercury   The Censor and Incense
The Altar   The Mirror

(23)

Preparation

[In the antechamber, finish with any private prayers or meditations. Move to the Laver and dip your hands in it. Say:]

'So therefore, first the Priest who governeth the works of Fire, must sprinkle with the Water of the loud-resounding Sea.'[271]

[Wipe some of the lustral water across your closed eyes. Say:]

'The Paternal Mind hath sowed symbols in the Soul,[272] let me perceive those symbols and from them, the Good itself, where the Father of all things resides.'[273]

[Take up your robe and put it on. Say:]

'Having put on the completely armed vigour of resounding Light, with triple strength fortifying the Soul and the Mind, I must put into the Mind the various Symbols, and not walk dispersedly on the empyraean path, but with concentration'.[274]

---

271 Chaldean Oracles I93 (hereafter CO), using the Westcott edition's translation and numbering. The modern Majercik numeration will be given in the footnotes. CO 133.

272 CO 80, 108(?).

273 CO 11. This does not appear in the Westcott edition.

274 CO 170, 2.

(24)

[Take the Lamen from its wrappings and raise it on high with both hands. Say:]

'All things are governed and subsist in this Triad: Faith, Truth, and Love.'[275]

[Put on the Lamen. Say:]

'Let the immortal depth of my Soul lead me earnestly upwards.'[276]

[Put on the Cloak. Say:]

'Stoop not down unto the Darkly-Splendid World; wherein continually lieth a faithless Depth, and Hades wrapped in clouds, delighting in unintelligible images, precipitous, winding, a black ever-rolling Abyss; ever espousing a Body unluminous, formless and void.'[277]

[Lower the hood. Say:]

'For I am furnished with every kind of Armour.'[278]

[Draw the Sword from its sheath and raise it with both hands on High. Say:]

---

275 CO 32, 48. "Faith, Truth, and Love" from CO 46. The latter does not appear in the Westcott edition.

276 CO 173, 112.

277 CO 145, 163.

278 CO 171, 72.

(25)

'Unto the Intellectual Whirlings of Intellectual
Fire, let all things be subservient, through the
persuasive counsel of the Father,[279] and let
me be amongst the guardians of the works of
the Father, and of the One Mind.'[280]

[When ready, enter the Priory.]

Purification and Consecration

[Move to the East and raise the Sword. Announce:]

'Procul, O procul este, profane!'

[Move to the West. Place the Sword at this point of
greatest darkness. Lay the Sword as though it were
blocking the passage of any Power of darkness. Take the
Chalice and purify the Priory with water. Return
the Chalice and take up the Incense. Consecrate the
Priory with fire. Return the Incense.]

[Retrieve the Sword and perform the Banishment
of the Flames of Prometheus. Return the Sword and
with the Ruby Ankh perform the Supreme Invoking
Ritual of the Ankh of Mercury. When complete, stand
West of the altar, facing East. Say:]

'O Lord of heaven and earth, creator and Maker
of all things visible and invisible, I, though
unworthy, by your assistance call upon you,
through your great messenger, the light of

---

279 CO 63, 81.
280 CO 41, 82(?).

(26)

the eternal sun, that you will give me your divine Spirit, to direct me in your truth to all good. Amen.

Because I earnestly desire to know the Arts of this life and such things that are necessary for us, which are so overwhelmed in darkness, and polluted with infinite human opinions, that I of my own power can attain to no knowledge in them unless you teach me. Grant me, therefore, one of your spirits, who may teach me those things which you would have me to know and learn, to your praise and glory, and the profit of our neighbor. Give me also an apt and teachable heart, that I may easily understand those things which you will teach me, and may hide them in my understanding, that I may bring them forth as out of your inexhaustible treasures, to all necessary uses. And give me grace, that I may use such thy gifts humbly, with awe and trembling, through your great messenger, the light of the eternal sun, with thy divine Spirit. Amen.[281]

Omnipotent and eternal God, who ordained the whole creation for your praise and glory, and for human reintegration, I beseech you to send your Spirit Per Deum of the Mercurial order, who shall inform and teach me those things which I shall ask of him and do all that I command. Nevertheless, not my will be done, but yours, through your great messenger, the light of the eternal sun.'[282]

---

281 Adapted from the Arbatel of Magic, Aphorism 21.
282 Adapted from Aphorism 21.

(27)

Evocation of Pulchitudo Dei

[Move to place the altar between yourself and the place of Mercury. Face the direction of Mercury. Say:]

'I do invocate and conjure you, O Spirit PVLCHIT-VDO DEI; and being with power armed from the Supreme Majesty, I do strongly command you by PVLCHITVDO DEI, QVIS VT DEVS, MENDICVS DEI, and the ARCHANGELI; by the most Powerful name of the Lord, the holy archangels, and choirs of angels, and by the very Word of God, I do invoke you, and by invocating conjure you. And being armed with power from the Supreme Majesty, I do strongly command you, by Him Who spake and it was done, and unto whom all creation be obedient. Also, I, being made after the image and likeness of God, endowed with power from God, and created according unto His will, do I exorcise thee by that most mighty and powerful name of God, PVLCHITVDO DEI, strong and wonderful, O you Spirit PVLCHITVDO DEI. I command you by Him who spake the Word and His Fiat was accomplished and by all the names of God. By the names of the Lord God Most High, I do exorcise you and do powerfully command you, O PVLCHITVDO DEI, that you do forthwith appear to me here before this Circle, in that Triangle that has been made sacred to you, and in your true and holy guise. And by this ineffable name, PVLCHITVDO DEI, do I command you, at which being heard the elements are overthrown, the air is shaken, the sea runs back, the fire is

(28)

quenched, the earth trembles, and all the hosts of the celestials, terrestrials, and infernals do tremble together in awe. Wherefore come, O PVLCHITVDO DEI, forthwith and without delay, form any or all parts of the heavens wherever you may be and make rational and true answers to all things that I shall demand of you. Come peaceably, visibly, and affably, now and without delay, manifesting which I shall desire. For you are conjured by the name of the Living and True God, PVLCHITVDO DEI, the mighty archangels QVIS VT DEVS and MENDICVS DEI, wherefore fulfill my commands, and persist you therein to the end, and according to my interest, visibly and affably speaking with a voice clear and intelligible without any ambiguity.

Enter in, appear to me PVLCHITVDO DEI, for I have spoken your name, and answer me with your holy voice in order that I might hear clearly and unerringly all your holy wisdom. Appear to me in your symbolic and true forms in this sacred mirror of the Arte, placed as it is within the Triangle made sacred to you. Let your 100,000 legions be present at my command. Speak with me concerning the power of your holy mind that I may learn all of your holy arts.'

[In the skyring mirror, communicate with the Spirit. When finished, thank the Spirit and give this license to depart.]

(29)

License to Depart

'O PVLCHITVDO DEI, because you have diligently answered my demands, and have been very ready and willing to come at my call, I do license you to depart to your proper place, without causing harm or danger to anyone or anything. Depart then, I say, and be ready to come at my call, being duly exorcised and conjured by the sacred rites of magic. I charge you to withdraw peaceably and quietly, and the peace of PVLCHITVDO DEI be ever continued between you and me. Amen.'

[Perform the Supreme Banishing Ritual of the Ankh of Mercury. Perform the Banishment of the Flames of Prometheus. Consecrate and purify the Priory with fire and with water. Withdraw from the priory and carefully note everything that transpired between yourself and the Spirit.]

The Rite is Complete

(30)

The CIRCLE of the ART

(31)

The TRIANGLE of the ART

BIBLIOGRAPHY

CEREMONIAL MAGIC

Blitz, K.T., Edouard, editor. *Ritual and Monitor of the Martinist Order*. Supreme Council of the M.O. for the U.S. of A, Order Kabbalistique de Rose + Croix, 1896.

Bogaard, Milko. "Manifestations of the Martinist Order." *Omega Nexus Online*, Feb. 2005, omeganexusonline.net/rcmo/martinistorders.htm. Accessed 22 Jan. 2016.

Butler, W.E. *Magic and the Magician*. Aquarian Press, 1991.

Crowley, Aleister. *Magic in Theory and Practice*, Dover Publications, 1976, pp. xii.

Davis, Kevin L. "Brothers from another Mother: The Historical Connection between Martinism and Freemasonry." Georgia Lodge of Research, May 2014, Kennesaw Lodge 33, Marietta, GA. https://www.academia.edu/9202075/Brothers_From_Another_Mother_The_Historical_Connection_Between_Martinism_and_Freemasonry. Accessed 19 Jan. 2016.

de Pasqually, Martinez. *Treatise on Reintegration of Beings*. Internet Archive. archive.org/details/treatise-on-the-reintegration-of-beings-martines-de-pasqually. Accessed 21 Oct. 2023.

Farrell, Nick. *King Over the Water: Samuel Mathers and the Golden Dawn*. Dublin, Kerubim Press, 2012.

Gilbert, R. A. *The Golden Dawn Scrapbook: The Rise and Fall of a Magical Order*. Samuel Weiser, Inc., 1997.

—. *The Golden Dawn: Twilight of the Magicians*. The Aquarian Press, 1983.

Godwin, Joscelyn, et al. *The Hermetic Brotherhood of Luxor: Initiatic and Historical Documents of an Order of Practical Occultism.* Samuel Weiser, Inc., 1995.

Greer, Mary K. *Women of the Golden Dawn: Rebels and Priestesses.* Park Street Press, 1995.

Hanegraaf, Wouter J. "Magic I: Introduction." *Dictionary of Gnosis and Western Esotericism,* Leiden, Brill, 2006, pp. 716.

King, Francis. *Modern Ritual Magic: The Rise of Western Occultism.* Dorset: Prism Press, 1989.

—. editor. *The Secret Rituals of the O.T.O.* Samuel Weiser, Inc., 1973.

Küntz, Darcy. *The Golden Dawn Source Book.* Holmes Publishing Group, 1996.

Majercik, Ruth, translator. *The Chaldean Oracles.* Wiltshire, Prometheus Trust, 2013.

"National Library of Ireland." *National Library of Ireland,* www.nli.ie. Accessed 21 Oct. 2023.

Peterson, Joseph. *Twilit Grotto: Archives of Western Esoterica.* Revised 4 Mar. 2023. www.esotericarchives.com/. Accessed 21 Oct. 2023.

Polychronis, Demetrius G. *An Anthology of Theurgic Operations of the Rose + Croix of the Orient.* Translated by Demetrius G. Polychronis, 3rd ed., Rose + Croix of the Orient, 2008. *The Masonic Trowel,* www.themasonictrowel.com/ebooks/freemasonry/eb0021.pdf. Accessed 22 Jan. 2016.

Randolph, Paschal Beverly and Maria de Naglowska. *Magia Sexualis: Sexual Practices for Magical Power.* Translated by Donald Traxler, Inner Traditions, 2012.

Ravignat, Mathiew G. *The Original High Degrees and Theurgical System of the Masonic Elect Cohen Knights of the Universe.* Lulu, 2019.

Regardie, Israel and John Michael Greer. *The Golden Dawn: The Original Account of the Teachings, Rites, and Ceremonies of the Hermetic Order.* Llewellyn Worldwide, 2016.

Waite, Arthur Edward. *Saint-Martin: The French Mystic and the Story of Modern Martinism.* William Rider & Son, 1922.

Westcott, William Wynn, editor. "The Chaldæn Oracles of Zororaster." 1895. *Twilit Grotto: Archives of Western Esoterica,* Joseph H. Peterson editor, digital edition, 1999, www.esotericarchives.com/oracle/oraclez.htm, Accessed 20 Jul. 2023.

Zalewski, Pat. *Golden Dawn Rituals and Commentaries.* Rosicrucian Order of the Golden Dawn, 2010.

FRATERNAL SOCIETIES

Bullock, Steven C. *Revolutionary Brotherhood: Freemasonry and the Transformation of the American Social Order, 1730–1840.* Omodundro Institute of Early American History and Culture and University of North Carolina Press, 1996.

Carnes, Mark C. *Secret Ritual and Manhood in Victorian America.* Yale University Press, 1989.

Evans, Henry Ridgley. *The History of the York and Scottish Rite in Freemasonry.* Kessinger Publishing, 2010.

Hogan, Timothy. *The Way of the Templar: A Manual for the Modern Knight Templar.* 2015.

Mackenzie, Kenneth. *The Royal Masonic Cyclopaedia.* Wellingborough, The Aquarian Press, 1987.

Mackey, Albert. *Encyclopedia of Freemasonry, Revised and Enlarged Edition,* vol. I. Chicago: The Masonic History Company, 1929.

—. *Encyclopedia of Freemasonry, Revised Edition,* vol. II. The Masonic History Company, 1921.

—. *The History of Freemasonry.* Gramercy Books, 1996.

McIntosh, Christopher. *The Rosicrucians: The History, Mythology, and Rituals of an Esoteric Order.* Samuel Weiser, Inc., 1997.

McIntosh, Christopher and Donate Pahnke McIntosh, translators. *Fama Fraternitatis: Manifesto of the Most Praiseworthy Order of the Rosy Cross, addressed to all the rulers, estates and learned of Europe.* Bremen, Vanadis Texts, 2014.

Pike, Albert. *Morals and Dogma of the Ancient and Accepted Scottish Rite of Freemasonry.* Supreme Council of the Thirty-Third Degree, Southern Jurisdiction of the United States, 1906.

Révauger, Cécile. *Black Freemasonry: From Prince Hall to the Giants of Jazz.* Inner Traditions, 2016.

"The Templar Uniforms." *Traveling Templar,* 19 Jan. 2012, www.travelingtemplar.com/2012/01/templar-uniforms.html. Accessed 25 Apr. 2016.

Zeldis, Leon. "An Esoteric View of the Rose-Croix Degree." *Pietre-Stones Review of Freemasonry,* www.freemasons-freemasonry.com/zeldis11.html. Accessed 2 May 2016.

Paganism

Carr-Gomm, Philip. *Druidcraft: The Magic of Wicca and Druidry.* Thorsons, 2002.

Dayan, Joan. *Haiti, History, and the Gods.* University of California Press, 1998.

Davis, Owen. *Popular Magic: Cunning-folk in English History.* London, Hambledon Continuum, 2007.

Desmangles, Leslie G. *The Faces of the Gods: Vodou and Roman Catholicism in Haiti.* The University of North Carolina Press, 1992.

Evans-Wentz, Walter Yeeling. *The Fairy-Faith in Celtic Countries.* Okitoks Press, 2017

Greer, John Michael. "What is the Druid Revival?" *Ancient Order of Druids in America,* 2003, aoda.org/publications/articles-on-druidry/druidrevival/. Accessed 5 Feb. 2016.

"Haitian Vodou Beliefs." *Vodou Religion,* www.vodoureligion.com/2011/04/haitian-Vodou-beliefs/. Accessed 22 Feb. 2016.

Heselton, Philip. *Witchfather: A Life of Gerald Gardner, Vol 1: Into the Witch Cult.* Leicestershire, Thoth Publications, 2012.

—. *Witchfather: A Life of Gerald Gardner. Vol 2: From Witch Cult to Wicca.* Leicestershire, Thoth Publications, 2012.

Hutton, Ronald. *Blood and Mistletoe: The History of the Druids in Britain.* Yale University Press, 2011.

—. *The Triumph of the Moon: A History of Modern Pagan Witchcraft.* Oxford University Press, 1999.

Kirk, Robert and Marina Warner. *The Secret Commonwealth of Elves, Fauns, and Fairies.* New York Review Books, 2007.

Lebor Gabála Érenn: Book of the Taking of Ireland, Part 1-5. Translated by R.A.S. Macalister. Irish Texts Society, 1941. *Celtic Literature Collective,* www.maryjones.us/ctexts/leborgabala. html. Accessed 5 Feb. 2016.

Morganwg, Iolo. *Barddas; or A Collection of Original Documents, Illustrative of the Theology, Wisdom, and Usages of the Bardo-Druidic System of the Isle of Britain.* Edited by J. William Ab Ithel, vol. I, London, 1874. *Internet Sacred Texts Archives,* John B. Hare, editor, 6 Nov. 2005 www.sacred-texts.com/neu/celt/bim1/index.htm. Accessed 5 Feb. 2016.

—. *Barddas; or A Collection of Original Documents, Illustrative of the Theology, Wisdom, and Usages of the Bardo-Druidic System of the Isle of Britain.* Edited by J. William Ab Ithel, vol. II, London, 1874. *Internet Sacred Texts Archives,* John B. Hare, editor, 6 Nov. 2005. www.sacred-texts.com/neu/celt/bim2/index.htm. Accessed 5 Feb. 2016.

Nichols, Ross. *The Book of Druidry: History, Sites and Wisdom.* London, Aquarian Press, 1992.

Pennick, Nigel. *Witchcraft & Secret Societies of Rural England: The Magic of Toadmen, Plough Witches, Mummers, and Bonesmen.* Rochester, Destiny Books, 2019.

Rankine, David, editor. *The Grimoire of Arthur Gauntlet: A 17th century London Cunning-man's book of charms, conjurations and prayers.* London, Avalonia, 2011.

Strickland, Simon. "Churchill's Druids and Britain's Satanic Prime Minister." *Simon's Obscure Pages,* www.angelfire.com/weird2/obscure2/druid.html. Accessed 5 Feb. 2016.

Toland, John. *History of the Druids.* Edited by R. Huddleston. Montrose, 1814.

Von Schnurbein, Stefanie. *Norse Revival: Transformations of Germanic Neopaganism.* Leiden: Brill, 2016.

Wawn, Andrew. "The Viking Revival." *BBC,* www.bbc.co.uk/history/ancient/vikings/revival_01.shtml. Accessed 8 Feb. 2016.

Yeats, William Butler, editor. *Fairy and Folk Tales of the Irish Peasantry.* London, 1888. *Internet Sacred Text Archive,* J.B. Hare, editor, www.sacred-texts.com/neu/yeats/fip/index.htm. Accessed 8 Feb. 2016.

Yeats, William Butler. *The Celtic Twilight*. London, 1902. *Internet Sacred Text Archive*, J.B. Hare, editor, 2004, www.sacred-texts.com/neu/yeats/twi/index.htm. Accessed 8 Feb. 2016.

—. "Ideas of Good and Evil: Magic." *The Hermetic Library*, 13 May 2017, hermetic.com/yeats/ideas-of-good-and-evil/magic.html. Accessed 8 Feb. 2016.

SPIRITUALISM

Braude, Ann. *Radical Spirits: Spiritualism and Women's Rights in Nineteenth-Century America*. Beacon Press, 1989.

Brown, Henry Harrison. *New Thought Primer: Origin, History and Principles of the Movement*. "Now" Folk, 1903.

Conan Doyle, Arthur. *The History of Spiritualism: Volumes I and II*. Arno Press, 1975. 2 vols.

Kontou, Tatiana, and Sarah A. Willburn. *The Ashgate Research Companion to Nineteenth-Century Spiritualism And The Occult*. Surrey, Ashgate, 2012.

Owen, Alex. *The Darkened Room: Women, Power, and Spiritualism in Late Victorian England*. University of Pennsylvania Press, 1990.

Weisberg, Barbara. *Talking to the Dead: Kate and Maggie Fox and the Rise of Spiritualism*. HarperSanFrancisco, 2004.

Wollstonecraft, Mary. *Vindication of the Rights of Women*. core.ac.uk/download/pdf/36679668.pdf. Accessed 18 October 2023.

STEAMPUNK AND AESTHETICS

"Chapter Three: Ipsissimus." *The Irregulars*, created by Tom Bidwell, season 1, episode 3, Drama Republic, 2021.

"Creating a Steampunk Persona." *Cowford Steampunk Society Wiki*, cowfordsteampunksociety.wikia.com/wiki/Creating_a_Steampunk_persona. Accessed 15 Feb. 2016.

Grieser, Alexandra and Jay Johnston. "What is an *Aesthetics of Religion?* From the Senses to Meaning—and Back Again." *Aesthetics of Religion*, edited by Alexandra Grieser and Jay Johnston, De Gruyter, 2017, pp. 1–49.

Hewitt, Jema Emilly Ladybird. *Steampunk Tea Party: Cakes & Toffees to Jams & Teas*. Cincinnati, David & Charles, 2013.

JRRL. "What is Steampunk?" *Steampunk.com*, web.archive. org/web/20190209143619/http://www.steampunk.com/ what-is-steampunk/. Accessed 21 Oct. 2023.

Sirkin, Austin. "How to Create a Steampunk Persona." Wonder-HowTo.com, http://steampunk.wonderhowto.com/how-to/ create-steampunk-persona-0138997/. Accessed 15 Feb. 2016.

Slade, Arthur. "Steampunk as Aesthetic." *Steampunk Scholar*, steampunkscholar.blogspot.com/p/aesthetic-101.html. Accessed 24 Feb. 2016.

Theosophy

"Annie Besant." *Varanasi.org.in*, https://www.varanasi.org.in/ annie-besant, Accessed 13 Dec. 2022.

Cranston, Sylvia. *H. B. P.: The Extraordinary Life & Influence of Helena Blavatsky, Founder of the Modern Theosophical Movement*. New York, Putnam, 1993.

de Purucker, G. "Encyclopedic Theosophical Glossary." *Theosophical University Press*, 1999 www.theosociety.org/pasadena/ etgloss/etg-hp.htm. Accessed. 7 Dec. 2015.

Gordon, J. S. *The Path of Initiation: Spiritual Evolution and the Restoration of the Western Mystery Tradition*. Inner Traditions, 2013.

Gomes, Michael. *The Dawning of the Theosophical Movement*. The Theosophical Publishing House, 1987.

Lavoie, Jeffrey D. *The Theosophical Society: The History of a Spiritualist Movement*. BrownWalker Press, 2012.

Murphet, Howard. *Hammer on the Mountain: Life of Henry Steel Olcott (1832–1907)*. Theosophical Publishing House, 1972.

Olcott, Henry Steel. *Old Diary Leaves: The History of the Theosophical Society*. Vol. 1, Theosophical Publishing House, 1974.

Prothero, Stephen R. *The White Buddhist: The Asian Odyssey of Henry Steel Olcott*. Indiana University Press, 1996.

INDEX